FIGHTING AN INVISIBLE ENEMY

FIGHTING AN INVISIBLE ENEMY

The Story of the National Institute for Communicable Diseases

BARRY SCHOUB

WITS UNIVERSITY PRESS

Published in South Africa by:
Wits University Press
1 Jan Smuts Avenue
Johannesburg 2001

www.witspress.co.za

First published 2024

http://dx.doi.org.10.18772/12024078974

978-1-77614-897-4 (Paperback)
978-1-77614-898-1 (Hardback)
978-1-77614-899-8 (Web PDF)
978-1-77614-900-1 (EPUB)

This publication is peer reviewed following international best practice standards for academic
and scholarly books.

Project manager: Inga Norenius
Copyeditor: Alison Lowry
Proofreader: Lisa Compton
Indexer: Margaret Ramsay
Cover design: Hothouse
Cover image: Guy Hall, the NICD BSL 4 lab at the Centre for Emerging Zoonotic and
Parasitic Diseases, courtesy of the National Health Laboratory Service
Typeset in 10 point Minion Pro

To the most wonderful NICD team, past and present. It has been a privilege, a pleasure and an honour working with all of you. This book is dedicated to your deep commitment to bettering the health of the country and contributing to global health.
May the NICD receive the support it so richly deserves to enable it to continue to grow to fulfil its sacred mission.

CONTENTS

FIGURES

FOREWORD

On a hot summer's morning just over 30 years ago, I drove through the gates of the National Institute for Virology (NIV) for my first meeting with Professor Barry Schoub. As I entered, the institute looked austere and its tight security foreboding, in sharp contrast to the smiling welcome from Schoub as he greeted me and then escorted me to his office for a meeting regarding vaccines. The institute was world renowned for its work on polio vaccines and haemorrhagic fevers in its biosafety level 4 (BSL-4) laboratory. As it was subsequently expanded and renamed as the National Institute for Communicable Diseases (NICD), it stood as a citadel of science against the threat Africa faced from existing and emerging infectious diseases.

Infectious diseases and pandemics remain major challenges to achieving the United Nations' Sustainable Development Goals by 2030, especially in Africa. To combat these threats, governments usually establish public health institutions, which bring together scientists and public health practitioners. The principal goal is to undertake surveillance and research in order to provide information and advice to policymakers on how to deal with these diseases.

Covid-19 catapulted the NICD into the public eye. From the first case in South Africa, it provided daily statistics on cases and deaths as well as scientific information to guide the country's pandemic response. While the NICD, as South Africa's public health agency or institution, may have risen to prominence in response to the Covid-19 pandemic, it was already well known for its track record in infectious diseases, most recently epitomised by its investigation of the country's listeriosis outbreak in 2017. Although the reputation of the NICD went well beyond South Africa's borders – through, for example, the assistance it provided to countries in West Africa during their Ebola outbreaks – its rich history is not widely known. This authoritative account of how the NICD of today came into existence, told by the virologist at the heart of its creation, remedies that gap.

Barry Schoub vividly captures how Professor James Gear's research and development of a polio vaccine led to the initial creation of the Poliomyelitis Research Foundation (PRF) in the 1950s. Resourced from the 'march of the tickeys' (based on the very successful 'march of dimes' initiative for polio fundraising in the US), the foundations were laid for the government subsequently to create the NIV, which merged decades later in 2002 with the South African Institute for Medical Research (SAIMR) to become the NICD. The book is not simply a story about science in laboratories; it is much more than that. One focus, for example, and something that is eloquently described in this narrative by Schoub, is on the fundamental challenge of the academic-government tension that faces almost all public health institutions across the globe.

Most of the professionals working in public health institutions function best in the academic paradigm, which comprises a high level of collegial autonomy, minimal layers of bureaucratic approval, and the freedom to exercise scientific curiosity in their research. This is in stark contrast to civil service institutions, which operate in strict hierarchical order and whose systems are designed to foster multiple layers of bureaucracy to ensure conformity and frustrate flexibility. Public health institutions all over the world face this balancing act of fostering science and discovery within the context of stifling government procedures. The predecessors of the NICD felt this tension tangibly right from the start. Being part of the government may provide the security of funding, which is required for long-term planning and institutionalisation of data collection, but it comes at a high price, such as the need to obtain authorisation from bureaucrats when aiming to communicate public health information to the public. This academic-government tension continues to prevail in the NICD to this day. In this it is not alone. Public health agencies in several countries struggle with this friction, at least until they reach a state of tolerable homeostasis.

Using the example of the South African government's AIDS denialism during a critical time in South Africa's history, when science needed to prevail, Schoub illustrates the importance of public health institutions being able to challenge political authority. The NICD needed the autonomy to actively challenge the country's president. It is through such difficult times that institutions develop their character and resilience and the NICD was no exception.

While fighting the unseen enemy of microbes – viruses, bacteria and fungi – the NICD painstakingly developed a record of academic excellence. Such excellence does not happen by accident; it is a product of exceptional leadership. Schoub gives full credit to his predecessors, who were outstanding, both academically and administratively. Having built its solid foundations, in handing him the NICD baton they enabled him to grow the institute to greater heights in its fight against the unseen enemy.

Covid-19 created new imperatives related to pandemic preparedness and response for public health institutions across the world. Today, the NICD faces this huge new challenge amidst shrinking budgets, pressure to deliver, and increasing dysfunctionality in South Africa's public health-care system. As future pandemics loom, everyone, including scientists, public health practitioners, politicians and members of the public, will be rooting for the continued success of the NICD. May the future yet-to-be-written chapters continue to laud the NICD's successes in tackling local and global public health threats.

Salim S. Abdool Karim, FRS
Director: CAPRISA
CAPRISA Professor of Global Health: Columbia University
Special Advisor to the Director-General of the
World Health Organization

I have had the personal privilege, honour and pleasure of serving in the National Institute for Communicable Diseases (NICD) and its predecessor institutes – the South African Institute for Medical Research (SAIMR) and the National Insitute for Virology (NIV) – for close to four decades. After my involvement in creating the NICD and serving as its founding director, I retired from the institute and have watched it grow to its illustrious present.

As 2019 was coming to a close Covid-19 arrived, the most serious pandemic to afflict humankind since the devastating Spanish influenza of 1918/1919. Covid-19 ignited unprecedented interest in public health and especially as it pertains to communicable diseases. The NICD was at the forefront of informing the public and guiding the authorities during the pandemic.

It seems that there is broad interest in hearing the story of the NICD. A goodly number of my professional colleagues, past and present, as well as non-professional friends, have urged me to tell the story of this venerable institution. Colleagues in the fields of communicable diseases and public health have been curious to learn about the origins of the institute and what went into its development, its colourful history and the rocky road of the early days. Many of my clinical colleagues have been keen to understand what lies behind the advisories, the bulletins and the research emanating from the institute. During Covid-19, but also for many years in the past, the NICD has occupied a prominent position through various reports in the media generating widespread and extensive interest from the non-professional but informed public. I would venture that a number of good citizens driving past the gates of the institute on Modderfontein Road on the north-eastern outskirts of Johannesburg wonder what exactly lies on the other side of the fence, and what goes on behind the scenes in those buildings. It was to provide answers to this broad spectrum of interests that inspired me to write this book.

The NICD has an attractive website – www.nicd.ac.za – which very palatably communicates information on communicable diseases and updated data, making it readily accessible to the public. My intention in writing this book is to complement what is already a most commendable and effective medium for advising and keeping the public informed. I have also set out to narrate the history of this globally prominent public health institution. The history is a rich one, and the story of the NICD's development illustrates the challenges of overcoming both political and organisational hurdles. Wrestling with the functional need for independence and autonomy while at the same time contending with the governmental nervousness of outing potentially thorny or sensitive information is a core part of my narrative.

The activities of the institute are essentially scientific, but science is not at the forefront of this book; I have deliberately backpedalled on the science. I do not in any remote sense claim to have written a reference text on communicable diseases. In fact the speed of scientific advances in the biomedical sciences is now largely witnessing the demise of the classic textbook. With the science advancing and expanding at unprecedented speed, the dissemination of research findings has also advanced considerably. Two online publications, medRxiv and bioRxiv, established by Yale University, are now widely used by scientists to expedite this dissemination. The publications serve as vehicles to get research findings out to the scientific community as quickly as possible. After an initial preliminary vetting, submissions are published on the website, thus bypassing the conventional cumbersome and time-consuming peer-review process. The research findings are generally subsequently submitted for publication to scientific journals.

As I will describe in the introduction, many public health institutions commenced with very humble beginnings. The NICD's big sister institution in the US, for instance, the Centers for Disease Control (CDC), began life as a malaria and tropical diseases research station shortly after the Second World War.[1] Similarly, the NICD's predecessors were incarnated as laboratories to respond to a specific public health problem. In the case of the South African Institute for Medical Research (SAIMR), this was to carry out research into pneumonia in the mines; the Poliomyelitis Research Foundation (PRF) was to do the same for polio.[2]

The chain of events that led to the establishment of the NICD is a tale of the art of lobbying and negotiating through an intimidating maze of civil service bureaucracy. Importantly, it is a lesson in how not to be discouraged by disappointments and setbacks during the process. The final result came to be a reference public health institution for communicable diseases on the southern tip of the African continent, a world-class centre of expertise in communicable diseases, an international partner to global health authorities, and a knowledge resource for the professional and the general public.

Crucially, successful management of communicable diseases is reliant on public health support which, in turn, is reliant on public knowledge that is founded on authentic, evidence- and data-based good science.[3] The all-pervasive social media of the modern era, as valuable as it is as a mass communication tool, has also, unfortunately, facilitated and promoted the insidious growth of anti-science, which has become a significant challenge to public health.[4] The pernicious anti-science lobby has grown from frivolous teatime talk to threats against the lives of scientists. Dr Anthony Fauci, one of the most prominent international commentators on communicable diseases, and adviser to seven US presidents, had to be provided with an armed security detail following threats to himself and his family during the Covid-19 pandemic. I, myself, have not escaped receiving offensive and abusive emails.

Before telling the story of the institute, it is incumbent on me to pay tribute to the founding fathers of the NICD, three giants in the field of communicable diseases in South Africa – Professor James Gear, Professor Hendrik Koornhof and Professor Wally Prozesky.

The famous statement on scientific progress made by Sir Isaac Newton in his letter to Robert Hook in 1675 – 'If I have seen further, it is by standing on the shoulders of giants'[5] – rings true when it comes to the evolution of the NICD and it has been an inspiring personal maxim for me. The NICD of today is a monumental tribute to the three communicable diseases pioneers in South African history who laid the foundations of the NICD, and on whose visionary efforts the NICD was built. I had the privilege of learning from all three mentors.

Professor James Gear was director of the SAIMR from 1960 to 1973. In addition, he was the director of the PRF, the predecessor of the NIV. Gear's role in pioneering the development of the polio vaccine, in the face of stern opposition from the medical establishment of the day, is described more fully in Chapter 1. Gear the man is best characterised by an appreciation written by Professor Jack Metz (a subsequent director of the SAIMR) and myself in the *South African Medical Journal*: 'In spite of all his honours and achievements, he is a humble, modest man. He is one of the greats in world medicine, yet he has remained a compassionate doctor who cares about the sick.'[6]

Professor Hendrik Koornhof, the head of the Department of Medical Microbiology at the SAIMR from 1960 until his retirement in 1992, was the trailblazer of the microbiology arm of the NICD. His encyclopaedic knowledge of microbiology was legendary, and under his watch the microbiology department grew into the largest medical microbiology centre in the country. It joined the NICD in 2002. I wrote a tribute to Professor Koornhof in a 2007 festschrift in his honour: 'To one of the great sons of South Africa – a remarkably knowledgeable biomedical scientist, an outstanding teacher and mentor . . . Perhaps the finest tribute that could be paid to Professor Koornhof is a legacy of so many distinguished careers throughout the world that he helped to create.'[7]

The third of the NICD pioneers was Professor O.W. (Wally) Prozesky, the first director of the NIV, who served from April 1976 until May 1982. On a personal note, he was the supervisor of my first doctoral thesis. A brilliant virologist, Prozesky pioneered the discipline of medical virology in South Africa. It was his vision and foresight and his lobbying in the halls of government that gave rise to the NIV. It was also his efforts and dedication which ensured that medical virology became a registrable specialist discipline in South Africa. I am deeply grateful for the personal interest he took in me when I arrived on his doorstep as a young inexperienced specialist microbiologist. He took me under his expert wing and played a pivotal role in launching and developing my career as a medical virologist.

I am often asked the question (and I am sure this is also true with many of my colleagues): if I were to have it all over again, would I have chosen the same career path? Of course a range of responses to this ubiquitous question can be made, but I will say this: I certainly would have chosen the same path again. It is with great gratitude that I acknowledge my good fortune in being part of a wonderful team of professionals in both the NIV and the NICD.

The health sciences, more than any of the other sciences, often tread a very sensitive, controversial and, not infrequently, fractious path. The Covid-19 pandemic in particular generated a great deal of heated controversy even among health professionals themselves. During the pandemic, I served as chairperson of the country's Ministerial Advisory Committee (MAC) on Covid-19 Vaccines (VMAC) almost a decade after I had retired from the NICD. This frequently placed me in the centre of the Covid-19 turbulence, some of which was intra-professional turbulence and is mentioned in Chapter 8.

It is important to end by saying that the opinions expressed in this book are my own and do not necessarily reflect the opinions of the NICD or any of its personnel. I take full personal responsibility for them.

ACKNOWLEDGEMENTS

The initial suggestion and encouragement to write a book on the history of the NICD came some years back, from Professor Jack Metz, the former director of the SAIMR, who himself had just published a book on the history of that institute. The current executive director of the NICD, Professor Adrian Puren, very kindly agreed to review the manuscript and made a number of valuable suggestions. We have had several useful discussions on the NICD and he also assisted in generously providing me with important contributions to the book.

I was indeed honoured when Professor Salim Abdool Karim happily agreed to write the foreword to the book and I do wish to acknowledge the foundational support he has given to me personally and also to the NICD over the three decades that we have known each other and worked together.

My former personal assistant, Irma Latsky, could be depended upon to be, as always, an enthusiastic, friendly and hyper-efficient assistant. I knew I could also depend on the willing helpfulness and generosity of the professionals of the NICD in providing me with photographic material for the book – Monica Birkhead, Janusz Paweska, John Frean and Basil Brooke, as well as Guy Hall of the National Health Laboratory Service (NHLS).

My sincere thanks to Alastair Moffat, the chair of the Poliomyelitis Research Foundation, for permitting me to harvest much of the information on the early days of the PRF from the book *The History of the Poliomyelitis Foundation* by James HS Gear. I would like to also record my sincere thanks to Sir Peter Piot, recently retired director of the London School of Hygiene and Tropical Medicine, for permission to quote from correspondence he sent me in 1987, which I have mentioned in Chapter 2, and similarly, to Carolyn Williamson, professor of virology at the University of Cape Town, for correspondence mentioned in Chapter 6.

It has been a great pleasure working initially with Roshan Cader, the commissioning editor of Wits University Press, and subsequently with Inga Norenius, Alison Lowry and Kirsten Perkins, who steered the manuscript through to its publication phase. My sincere thanks also to Veronica Klipp, Wits University publisher, and also to my dear colleague Wits University Deputy Vice-Chancellor Lynn Morris, who enthusiastically encouraged the writing of this book when I first intimated the idea to her.

Finally, to my dear wife Barbara, who has strongly supported me through a long career at the NIV and NICD, and encouraged me to write the book when it was still only a vague vision. She reviewed the manuscript and made valuable suggestions. I am deeply grateful for her unstinting support and encouragement to her permanent student husband. The support also from our children, Wendy Kahn, Richard Schoub and Peter Schoub, and their families is immensely appreciated.

ACRONYMS AND ABBREVIATIONS

AFP	acute flaccid paralysis
AIDS	Acquired Immunodeficiency Syndrome
ART	antiretroviral therapy
ARV	antiretroviral
AZT	azidothymidine (also called zidovudine)
BSL-4	biosafety level 4
CAPRISA	Centre for the AIDS Programme of Research in South Africa
CCHF	Crimean-Congo haemorrhagic fever
CDC	Centers for Disease Control and Prevention
CHIVSTI	Centre for HIV and Sexually Transmitted Infections
cVDPV	Circulating Vaccine-Derived Poliovirus
DDG	deputy director general
DG	director general
DRC	Democratic Republic of the Congo
DREAMS	Determined, Empowered, AIDS-free, Mentored and Safe
FETP	Field Epidemiology and Training Programme
GAVI	Global Alliance for Vaccines and Immunization (now referred to as the GAVI Alliance)

GERMS-SA	South African Group for Enteric Respiratory and Meningeal Diseases
GPEI	Global Polio Eradication Initiative
HIV	human immunodeficiency virus
IANPHI	International Association of National Public Health Institutes
MMWR	*Morbidity and Mortality Weekly Report*
MRC	Medical Research Council
MSM	men who have sex with men
NHLS	National Health Laboratory Service
NICD	National Institute for Communicable Diseases
NIV	National Institute for Virology
PCR	polymerase chain reaction
PRF	Poliomyelitis Research Foundation
SAFELTP	South African Field Epidemiology and Laboratory Training Programme
SAIMR	South African Institute for Medical Research
SARS-CoV-2	Severe Acute Respiratory Syndrome Coronavirus -2
SAVP	South African Vaccine Producers
SPU	Special Pathogens Unit
STI	sexually transmitted infection
TAC	Treatment Action Committee
TB	tuberculosis
UNAIDS	Joint United Nations Programme on HIV/AIDS
WHO	World Health Organization

INTRODUCTION

U nseen enemies – germs invisible to the naked eye and viruses invisible even under the light microscope – have ravaged humankind since prehistoric days. The fight against them is waged on many fronts. Most visible is the family doctor prescribing antibiotics for Grandad's bronchitis. Largely invisible to the general public, however, are the public health institutions combating the invisible enemy behind the scenes. This work means that no one today wakes up saying, 'Thank goodness I don't have smallpox this morning'. This is the story of one such public health institution – the National Institute for Communicable Diseases (NICD) of South Africa.

Before recorded history there was already evidence of tuberculosis (TB) in the bones of prehistoric humans. The dreaded smallpox, a disease of great antiquity, was known to the ancient civilisations of China and India some twelve thousand years ago.[8] The ancient Hindi civilisations in India even had their own special smallpox deity – the Shri Sitala Devi. Clear evidence of the scourge is visible in the mummified head of Pharaoh Ramses V, 1160 BCE. Centuries later smallpox was to bring death and misery to the royalty of Europe, to world leaders of several countries of Europe and North America, and to millions of the common people throughout the world.

Similarly, the Justinian plague, during the reign of Emperor Justinian I (527–565 CE), killed millions and was a portent of the Black

Death catastrophe that swept through Europe some eight centuries later (1346–1352), and was estimated to have wiped out about one-third or more of the population of Europe.

These are but two examples of massive epidemics of communicable diseases, which continued to devastate human populations right up until the twentieth century. Between February 1918 and April 1920, three waves of the devastating Spanish influenza pandemic killed between 25 and 50 million people, considerably more than had died from the hostilities of the preceding Great War.

It is nearing a half-century since our vaccines eradicated smallpox from the planet; we are closing in on doing the same for polio and perhaps a few other communicable diseases. Modern medicine, advanced science and state-of-the-art technologies now appear to be able to deal pretty adequately with the communicable disease afflictions of yesteryear. But have we reached a stage, with the scientific armoury at our disposal, to be able to relax our vigilance? Are we done with communicable diseases?

The dawning of the twentieth century ushered in the modern scientific era for the physical and biological sciences. The outpouring of new discoveries and the rapidly increasing understanding of the natural world were greeted with euphoria. Technological advances were not far behind.

Following the great advances in physics in the late nineteenth and early twentieth centuries, it seemed that little else remained to be discovered. A confident Lord Kelvin, addressing the British Association for the Advancement of Science, remarked, in 1900, that 'there is nothing new to be discovered in physics'.[9] A similarly confident Albert Michelson, an American physicist who would go on to win a Nobel Prize in 1907, felt able to conclude in 1903: 'The more important fundamental laws and facts of physical science have all been discovered . . . our future discoveries must be looked for in the sixth place of decimals'.[10] Such overconfident optimism was soon shown, quite embarrassingly, to be overly hasty.

The story was not so different in the medical sciences, in particular in the realm of communicable diseases. Accompanying the gratifyingly rapid advances in the biomedical sciences, most specifically in infection control and prevention, many overconfident and optimistic assurances were made that the end of the era of communicable diseases was nigh. Henry Sigerist, the prominent Swiss-American medical historian, confidently predicted in 1931 that 'most of the communicable diseases have now yielded up their secrets . . . Many illnesses have been completely exterminated; others [have been brought] largely under control.'[11] Somewhat later, US Surgeon General William H. Stewart was said to have told Congress in 1969 (although this has subsequently been disputed by some historians) that it was time to 'close the book on communicable diseases'.[12]

When political expediency overtakes scientific knowledge, gaffes like these are often not far behind. Even as late as 1984, premature and overly optimistic predictions were still being made. Margaret Heckler, then US secretary of health and human services, promised the world in the year after the discovery of the HI virus that 'we hope to have an AIDS vaccine ready for testing in about 2 years'.[13] Forty years later an effective AIDS vaccine remains elusively not even on the horizon.

The apprehension and the dread of the earlier plagues steadily abated during the twentieth century as remarkable advances were made in preventing infectious diseases through vaccines and clean water, as well as the powerful tool of antibiotics for treating infectious diseases. Now it was non-communicable diseases – cardiovascular conditions, cancer and degenerative diseases – that came to be the prime concern of the industrialised, developed world.

However, two looming grave threats to human welfare have, in recent times, rekindled communicable diseases apprehension. The first is the growing frequency of outbreaks of new infectious diseases coming mainly from the animal kingdom, the so-called zoonoses. These include the much-feared formidable viral haemorrhagic fevers and the recent Covid-19 pandemic which shook the world with its global impact of sickness and death. The second threat is increasing bacterial resistance to antibiotics and, with it, the spectre of a future post-antibiotic world.

COMMUNICABLE DISEASES IN OUR WORLD OF TODAY

The place of communicable diseases in the gallery of illness and death in the world of today varies markedly according to a country's socio-economic level and also according to age. In high-income countries, communicable diseases are a smaller component of the burden of diseases and play second fiddle to non-communicable diseases.[14] The latter category is certainly the dominant cause of mortality in these countries, with cardiovascular diseases and cancer being the main contributors. In recent years, however, the global total of seven million deaths due to Covid-19 has somewhat tilted the balance towards communicable diseases, even in high-income countries. In low- to middle-income countries, in contrast, deaths from communicable diseases are common, and in some they are the dominant cause of death. For example, in Kenya the leading cause of death is infectious diarrhoeal disease, while in South Africa and Botswana HIV/AIDS claims the highest proportion of mortality.[15]

Age is an important determinant of the relative importance of communicable diseases throughout the world. While infant and child mortality has declined steeply in modern times, communicable diseases such as respiratory infections and diarrhoeal disease remain the dominant causes of death in this age group.

Preventive programmes and public health strategies for non-communicable diseases are different in many respects from those of communicable diseases. Prevention of non-communicable diseases is, in the main, focused on personal responsibilities, including lifestyle practices, preventive screening and promotion of healthy living.

With communicable diseases, prevention strategies are considerably wider. Personal responsibilities play a critical role here, too, in the form of hygiene routines, such as hand washing, respiratory etiquette, food hygiene and sexual practices. In addition, community, regional and national bodies are tasked with critical roles in the prevention and management of communicable diseases. Vigilant surveillance to be alerted to early warning signals of impending outbreaks, monitoring of prevention programmes such as vaccine coverage, detection of new infections or newly imported infections, and management of outbreaks are some of the crucial functions of a public health body such as the NICD.

PUBLIC HEALTH INSTITUTIONS

Science-based institutions for public health have been established in many countries throughout the world. As an indication, the International Association of National Public Health Institutes (IANPHI), as of December 2021, comprised 110 members in 95 countries throughout the world, benefiting over six billion people.[16]

Many of these public health institutions started life as small, often low-profile bodies, hardly known to exist by the general public. In a number of cases they commenced activities addressing only a single specific, well-circumscribed, disease-related public health problem. So, for example (as we will see in Chapter 1), the early seeds that gave rise to the NICD were planted specifically to address the high-profile poliomyelitis outbreaks in South Africa in the mid to late 1940s. The same narrative applies in the case of the largest public health institution in the world, the Centers for Disease Control and Prevention (CDC) in the US. That venerable institution began life shortly after the Second World War, in July 1946, to assist in the control of malaria and several other tropical and subtropical diseases.[17] From those humble beginnings, the CDC grew rapidly, from a staff complement of 369 employees to an impressive institution with a worldwide reach and 15 000 employees.

The life story of the NICD followed a similar paradigm. In chapters 1 and 2 I describe how the NICD grew rapidly from its very modest beginnings of some 70 employees of the Poliomyelitis Research Foundation (PRF), being responsible for a single infectious disease – namely, polio – through the stage of the National Institute for Virology (NIV), to the current NICD, with its current staff complement of well over 500 employees.

An essential responsibility of a public health institution is to provide recommendations and advisories based on scientific knowledge to the policymakers of the country. These science-based recommendations go on to make up one component of the considerations that contribute to evidence- and data-based public health decisions.

The functioning of the laboratories of the public health institution is somewhat differently focused compared to that of the clinical diagnostic laboratories. In both the private and the public hospital sectors, clinical diagnostic laboratories receive samples from patients for diagnostic testing and provide the results and interpretations to referring doctors. These laboratories interact with the practising doctor in the management of the patient, supplying supplementary laboratory information to support the clinical assessment.

Public health laboratories often also play a similar patient-oriented diagnostic role in receiving specimens from individual patients to provide laboratory support to doctors, but their mission is considerably broader. These laboratories' principal responsibilities would also include reference testing for more highly specialised investigations, as well as surveillance and monitoring, training and, to a large extent, applied research. In many public health laboratories, such as the CDC, the scope of activities covers all aspects of public health, well beyond communicable diseases. In others, such as the NICD, activities and interests are confined to communicable diseases.

VALIDATING SCIENCE – THE BEDROCK OF THE PUBLIC HEALTH INSTITUTION

In the modern world of mass electronic communication and all-pervasive social media, scientific facts and scientific reality are regularly being subverted by a war on science and scientific truth by an increasingly conspicuous anti-science voice.[18] It is more important than ever, therefore, to underline why orthodox science and the scientific process are the underpinnings of all activities in bodies such as public health institutions. The rules and regulations that govern the pursuit of science, which come from science-based organisations, are there to assure the authenticity and the validity of the data and information these operations produce.

The international network of scholarly endeavours in the sciences is immense – perhaps most strikingly exhibited by the vastness of the world of scientific publications. A study in 2014 in Canada found that in that year alone 2.5 million new scientific papers were published in 28 100 scholarly, peer-reviewed journals.[19] With a four to five per cent increase in the number of publishing scientists globally, the tally of publications today must be considerably greater. Furthermore, in the world of science the position of the biomedical sciences is particularly prominent. As an indication, in Chapter 8 I mention that 98 of the 100 most cited papers in 2020/2021, throughout all of the sciences, related to Covid-19 alone![20]

And yet, paradoxically, it is the science of medicine, more than any of the other sciences, that suffers from the most mistrust and scepticism among the general public. Of course, ownership of one's personal body and one's personal health is sacrosanct, and each person's privacy and integrity are enshrined in constitutional rights – and of course choice is paramount – but sadly, one must ask on what evidence do those who eschew medical science base their choices? Why is it that medical science is singled out so frequently for challenge by populist non-science? Few members of the public would question the aeronautical engineering science used for the design of the aircraft in which they fly, but when it comes to the medical sciences more than a handful of the public see themselves as self-styled and very confident 'experts' in health matters, be it vaccination or natural healing. The sad case of ivermectin during the Covid-19 era stands out as an example of this medical dissidence.[21] (The drug, an anti-parasitic agent used in veterinary medicine, demonstrated absolutely no evidence of efficacy against Covid-19 but did demonstrate solid evidence of its toxicity. Widespread international activism and lobbying, even involving senior political figures, failed to make inroads to stop the use of this material to treat Covid-19.)

COMMUNICATING SCIENCE – THE ROLE OF THE PUBLIC HEALTH INSTITUTION

The Covid-19 pandemic, in particular, demonstrated the critical importance of science communication in the interests of public health. A timely short leading article in the journal *Science* points out that in contrast to the 'breath-taking advances'[22] in science, the art of communicating complex and nuanced information has lagged behind. The scientific understanding of Covid-19 did change markedly during the course of the pandemic as research revealed an ongoing greater understanding of this new disease. Together with these changes in science, policy recommendations changed accordingly. Some examples were: the duration of isolation following infection from 12 to 7 days; the changing role of droplets versus aerosols as transmission vehicles; the effectiveness of masking; and several other amendments. Not surprisingly, communications during the Covid-19 pandemic necessarily reflected these changes in their messaging to the public, which changes at times led to some confusion. It also led, unfortunately, to a degree of mistrust and even to defiance of public health restrictions.

Unfortunately, public health communicators still struggle to achieve the ideal balance between brevity and simplicity on the one hand, and scientific accuracy and the ability to convey nuanced messaging effectively on the other. Hopefully, reflections on the Covid-19 pandemic will encompass lessons learned, including addressing the deficiency in communications, before the next public health challenge.

Along with many positive innovations the Covid-19 pandemic also laid bare a number of deficiencies. The prestigious medical journal *The Lancet* commissioned a team of distinguished international scientists throughout the world to review the management of the Covid-19 pandemic globally.[23] A 57-page document entitled 'The Lancet Commission on Lessons for the Future from the COVID-19 Pandemic' was produced and recently published in the journal.

FIGHTING THE UNSEEN ENEMY

The chimera is a creature from Greek mythology. It was purported to be a fire-breathing beast made up of the head of a lion, the body of a goat and the tail of a serpent. In the biological sciences, the term 'chimera' is used to describe a hybrid organism produced from the fusion of separate and different components of genetic material. The term can very aptly be used to define the NICD and its predecessor institutions – a hybrid creation of a scientific centre of excellence fused with a civil service organisation and serving a national purpose, often saddled with political overtones.

The tale of the NICD is generally one of a symbiotic and mutually productive chimera. However, it must be said that there have been challenges. In the beginning perhaps these could be put down to the growing pains of a developing institution – they were certainly more prominent in the earlier formative years of the institute. Not unexpectedly, blending a disparate mixture of scientists and medical professionals from academic backgrounds together with administrators from civil service backgrounds would be a significant challenge, and there were indeed rocky periods that needed to be negotiated. Each world had to find each other and establish the best of working relationships, which they eventually succeeded, reasonably satisfactorily, in achieving.

The very first challenge the chimera faced came with the impetus for the birth of the first predecessor institution, the PRF. In Chapter 1, which deals with the early seeds of the NICD, I describe how even at that stage the plans – to create a valuable medical asset to combat a serious health threat, namely, poliomyelitis – ran afoul of the authorities. The very idea and the concept of creating a facility to carry out research and produce a polio vaccine was vigorously opposed by the doctrinaire medical establishment of the time and an equally hard-nosed government. Fortunately, public anti-vaccination sentiment was rather muted in those days. Paradoxically, it was ultimately the public who came to the rescue of the venture; it was the person in the street who provided the support, both financially and in spirit.

Shortly after the eventual construction of the PRF, the serious public health threat of polio was eliminated from the country.

The successor of the PRF, the NIV, at its commencement, was fortunate to see a healthy synergism with the government of the day. It certainly helped that the government was fearful of the dreaded viral haemorrhagic fevers that were starting to be recognised and were growing in frequency in neighbouring African countries. However, the honeymoon did not last long. With the country involved in a war in neighbouring Namibia (then South West Africa) as well as on its own borders, the government became haunted by the spectre of biological weapons. It was this fear that led to its first political clash with the NIV. Waving the threat of smallpox as a biological weapon, the government prohibited the NIV for several months from destroying its remaining stocks of smallpox virus, as was demanded by the World Health Organization (WHO) and the international health community. This further aggravated the progressively intensifying academic isolation of the institute because of the apartheid policies of the government. To complement this political lodestone, administrative paranoia severely curtailed the freedoms of operation of the NIV. Controls on the activities of the institute were further tightened, reaching even to a micromanagement level.

The most overt clash between science and government involved the HIV/AIDS epidemic. Tragically, the government of the Mbeki era adopted an anti-science dissident position on the HIV/AIDS issue, which was led by the president himself. This needlessly delayed the availability of anti-retroviral therapy (ART), resulting in significant loss of life. The NICD was not immune to the resulting fallout. Scientists at the NICD and throughout the country suffered significant reputational damage in the international scientific arena. Precious resources of the NICD were also recklessly squandered on direct instructions from the government compelling the institute to carry out needless laboratory tests concocted by HIV dissidents who were brought to the country from abroad as guests of the government.

These irksome hiccups in the narrative of the NICD are now history. The present NICD chimera is a highly productive world-class public health institution and it plays a prominent role on the international stage of communicable diseases prevention. In addition to its national responsibilities of surveillance and monitoring, it is affiliated with several international health bodies such as the WHO and the CDC. The routine diagnostic activities, the epidemiological modelling operations, the field trips in the country and on the continent and, of course, the myriad highly productive research activities will be discussed in the following chapters.

1

The early seeds

The honoured parents who gave birth to the NICD were two venerable public health institutions. First came the esteemed South African Institute for Medical Research (SAIMR), and second, an equally esteemed but younger institution, the Poliomyelitis Research Foundation (PRF). Very soon after their individual births both institutions found themselves accountable for vastly more than their single disease responsibilities, pneumonia in the case of the former and poliomyelitis in the case of the latter.

With the SAIMR it was the wide spectrum of laboratory medicine, and with the PRF the wide array of viral diseases of humans.

THE SAIMR (1912–1999)

In 1912, just two years before the start of the First World War, the Chamber of Mines of South Africa, the employer organisation of the country's mining industry, provided funds for the creation of the SAIMR. Its mission was to carry out research into the various medical challenges facing the mining industry, most specifically pneumonia. The government of the day provided an equal amount of funding for the institute to be a facility to serve the population of the country as a whole.

Not long after the birth of the SAIMR, the First World War broke out and the institute was called on to provide medical support for the war effort. With the outbreak of the Second World War in 1939, the institute was again called on to provide medical support for the war effort. This saw a much greater demand on the institute. Supplies of yellow fever and typhus vaccines went north to the military and civilian populations of the African continent involved in the conflict, and the typhus vaccine was sent to the Soviet theatre of the war.

In the earliest days of the SAIMR, the needs of the mining industry ensured that a great deal of energy went into research on bacterial pneumonia, a huge problem among mining personnel at the time. The causative bacterium, the pneumococcus, was rigorously investigated, leading to the development of an effective preventive vaccine. This achievement earned a knighthood for the second director of the SAIMR, Sir Spencer Lister. Research in bacteriology expanded rapidly in the ensuing years, with significant findings being published on a variety of bacteria such as typhoid fever, whooping cough and plague.

The personnel of the SAIMR also provided the local University of the Witwatersrand with academic support and constituted the medical school's pathology departments. In 1970 the School of Pathology was created, with the director of the SAIMR, Professor Jack Metz, being appointed to head the school. The departments of microbiological pathology and tropical pathology would later, in 2002, join with the NIV to form the NICD.

For an extensive account of the earlier history of the SAIMR, the reader is referred to the volume written by Marais Malan entitled *In Quest of Health: The South African Institute for Medical Research 1912–1973*.[24] An equally extensive follow-up was written by Jack Metz, taking the history of the SAIMR forward from 1974 until the SAIMR was reorganised into the National Health Laboratory Service (NHLS) in 1999. It is entitled

South Africa's Health Sentinel: The South African Institute for Medical Research 1974 to 1999.[25]

POLIO AND THE PRF (1954–1976)

The feared disease of the 1940s and 1950s was polio.

Epidemics of poliomyelitis were almost unknown to the general public before the twentieth century (although the disease itself is depicted in an Egyptian stele dating back to the eighteenth dynasty 1403–1385 BCE). From 1900 onwards, major epidemics were experienced in Europe and North America, peaking in the 1940s and 1950s. In South Africa, epidemics were not recorded until 1918, coinciding with the end of the Great War and the return of South African troops from campaigns in the Middle East. Subsequently, there were no further outbreaks until the close of the Second World War when, again, the onset of epidemics coincided with troops returning to the country from the North African and Middle Eastern theatres of war. Major epidemics of poliomyelitis broke out throughout South Africa in 1944 and 1945.[26]

Although poliomyelitis as a public health challenge did not rank among the top causes of mortality and morbidity in South Africa, it nevertheless caused a great deal of consternation and alarm in the population. The mood of anxiety at the time in the country, as well as throughout the developed world, is perhaps best illustrated by Aaron Klein's book *Trial by Fury: The Polio Vaccine Controversy*, in which he writes: 'The outbreaks were accompanied by a great deal of emotional terror; not the mass hysteria which characterized the Black Plague of the 14th century, but a quiet dread in the minds of parents who lived with the fear that at any time poliomyelitis could paralyze or kill their children.'[27] Of relevance to the appeal for funds for research, it did not go unnoticed that the disease affected up to 10 times as many white people as black people, unlike, for example, tuberculosis, which constituted a vastly greater overall health burden, particularly in the African population.

13

Appealing for funds for polio vaccine research in South Africa

The most severe of the polio epidemics in South Africa, the third epidemic, took place in 1948 and resulted in some 3 000 paralytic cases and 200 deaths.[28] Intense alarm gripped the predominantly white middle and upper classes of South Africa. Against this background of apprehension in the population, Professor James Gear, who had been at the forefront of communicable diseases in general and now polio in particular, delivered a lecture at the medical school of the University of the Witwatersrand in Johannesburg. It was a lecture to medical professionals and was closed to the public, but a newspaper reporter was smuggled into the lecture by a medical student friend. After the lecture, the reporter contacted the then mayoress of the City of Johannesburg, Mrs Evelyn Gordon. He suggested to her that an appeal should be launched for funds for research into poliomyelitis with the aim of producing a preventive vaccine similar to that being developed in the US.

In the US the National Foundation for Infantile Paralysis was founded in 1938 by President Franklin D. Roosevelt, himself a victim of poliomyelitis. Among its many fundraising activities, it launched the famous 'March of Dimes' to collect funds from the public to combat polio.

In South Africa, the Polio Research Appeal similarly set about launching a variety of fundraising activities.[29] Two of the best-known drives were the 'March of Tickeys' – the South African coin at the time equivalent to the dime – and the 'Snowball Procession'. The latter was an initiative of the major theatre organisation of South Africa in those days, African Consolidated Theatres Limited. A well-known Hollywood actor, Donald O'Connor, who had campaigned for polio in the US, journeyed by sea to South Africa to take part in the various fundraising activities. The Snowball Procession was a cavalcade of cars emblazoned with the slogan 'Give Liberally to Fight Polio'. The procession with Donald O'Connor and several beauty queens (the 'Hollywood Beauties') journeyed through towns to the east and west of Johannesburg as well as through Johannesburg itself. The procession was met by the mayors of each of the towns and several thousand rapturous, predominantly white crowds.

A movie was commissioned featuring the superintendent of the Johannesburg Hospital and demonstrating footage of children with acute and convalescent polio. The movie's script passionately spelled out the suffering of affected children with their 'twisted limbs and paralyzed muscles, who would bear the marks of polio all their lives'. The superintendent made an emotional appeal for funds for the construction of the necessary laboratories, equipment and staff. The target was set at £500 000, a sum close to 15 per cent of the total Department of Health budget for that year. The public responded with great enthusiasm and the total was soon reached.

Opposition from the senior medical establishment

In contrast to this public enthusiasm, the response from the government, and even much of the medical fraternity, was far from encouraging. The *South African Medical Journal* in September 1955 published a letter from the Border branch of the Medical Association of South Africa (MASA), which was subsequently reprinted in the lay press and received widespread publicity:

> The Institute of Polio Research has produced a vaccine without any trial on humans, and without any knowledge at all of the long-term effects or the length of immunity conferred, and has decided to use it in mass vaccination . . . The Department is almost stampeding the public into having their children vaccinated with a vaccine the effects of which – and this is admitted – may even be harmful and dangerous . . . the local body of medical men [decided] to advise their patients not to submit to the vaccination with a vaccine the effects of which are questionable.[30]

An acrimonious exchange of correspondence took place between Professor Gear on the one hand, and Dr Maurice Shapiro (director of the South African Blood Transfusion Service) and Dr Hillel Shapiro (editor of the *South African Medical Journal* and another medical journal, *Medical Proceedings*) on the other. Both of these esteemed doctors vehemently opposed the administration of the polio vaccine to children. They felt that the research should rather be carried out in better-resourced countries like the US, and that South Africa should be focusing on local diseases which carried a much greater health burden, such as tuberculosis. This opinion was strongly supported by several senior members of the medical profession.

The Council for Scientific and Industrial Research (CSIR), South Africa's chief scientific research and development organisation, which was founded in 1945, got involved. Until the creation of the South African Medical Research Council (MRC) in 1969, this was the organisation responsible for the promotion and funding of medical research in the country. It invited the secretary of the Medical Research Council of Great Britain, Sir Edward Mellanby, who was in South Africa at the time, to advise on funding the development of a poliomyelitis vaccine in the country. After consulting experts in the United Kingdom, Sir Edward recommended against supporting the project, maintaining it was 'intellectual dishonesty'.[31]

The government's Department of Health, after receiving a great deal of negative comments about the polio vaccine, refused to provide financial support to the project.

It was not difficult to see that funding tuberculosis could be viewed as a far greater and immediate public health need, notwithstanding that it was pointed out that the responsible pathogen for tuberculosis had been identified and a cure was already available. It was true that polio, in those years, was a disease mainly affecting the more privileged members of the South African population. Nevertheless, at the same time poliomyelitis was a greater scientific research challenge and South Africa was in an ideal position to carry out the research needed to develop a preventive vaccine.

Success – the establishment of the PRF and the production of polio vaccine

With the collection of the necessary funding from public contributions to the Polio Research Appeal, a board of trustees was established to take the project forward, which board became the Poliomyelitis Research Foundation (PRF). It set about building laboratories on a site on the farm Rietfontein on the north-eastern outskirts of Johannesburg. The site had already housed the serum laboratories of the SAIMR and the stables for the horses used for making various antisera (for example, snakebite antisera).

The foundation stone for the building was laid by Mrs Gordon in July 1951 in her capacity as chairman of the executive committee of the PRF and, in 1953, the new state-of-the-art laboratories, dubbed the 'polio palace', were opened by the then minister of health. These buildings would in time form the core of the future NIV and, subsequently, the NICD.

In 1954 the first batches of locally produced polio vaccines were available for trial, making South Africa one of only four countries in the world to have developed its own vaccine. The project had been driven by one of the most eminent communicable diseases physicians in the country, James Gear, who was duly appointed as the first director of the PRF laboratories. The first batches made in these laboratories, and among the first used for human vaccination worldwide, were ready for use in 1955. They were initially tested on 12 children of members of the staff of the laboratories, including Gear's four sons.

South Africa became one of the first countries in the world to introduce universal polio immunisation for its population. Initially, this was the inactivated injected vaccine in the latter part of the 1950s; subsequently, the oral live vaccine was used in the early 1960s. Polio vaccination was made compulsory for all South African infants in 1963, using a vaccine made in the PRF laboratories.

Soon after its establishment, the laboratories broadened out beyond polio research and vaccine production and the PRF became the leading centre for viral diagnostics and research for the African continent.

The PRF board of trustees – the jewel of virology research in South Africa

The early days of the Polio Research Appeal of the late 1940s saw the ordinary person in the street contribute generously to the funding of medical research. The board of trustees of the PRF looked after and administered the funds, which were used for the construction of the research and viral diagnostic laboratories, as well as the construction of the facilities for the production of polio and other viral vaccines.

Members of the appeal as well as members of the board were all volunteers who gave freely of their time, energy and expertise. The major portion of the current 10-member board is comprised not of health professionals but private individuals and senior members of the business and finance sectors of the public.

The investment sub-committee of the PRF very successfully managed the funds and continues to do so to this day, with its members giving selflessly of themselves to promote research into viral diseases. The financial difficulties in doing medical research in South Africa caused by the currency weakness of the South African rand is reflected in the values of the assets of the PRF over the years related to the US dollar. Excellent investment strategies by the sub-committee saw its assets grow 138-fold from R1.3 million in 1976 to R179 million in 2019. However, in US dollar terms it has only grown nine-fold, from the equivalent US$1.498 million in 1976 to US$13.531 million in 2019.

The cost of administration of the funds has been kept to an absolute minimum, with the members of the board of trustees receiving no remuneration. This has enabled the foundation to disburse research grants, now averaging R12 million annually, to further research into viral diseases and to build capacity in the discipline of virology.[32]

Supporting the board of trustees is a scientific advisory panel made up of the heads of virology departments of all the country's medical schools together with additional experts in the field. This committee provides necessary professional advice and is responsible for reviewing grant applications and making recommendations to the board for the awarding of grants.

2

The National Institute for Virology

B y the mid 1970s the responsibility and financial burden of maintaining
the rapidly expanding laboratories of the PRF was becoming too much
of a burden for the board of trustees and approaches were made to the
Department of Health to purchase the laboratories and take over their governance. The timing of the negotiations, which led to the official establishment of the NIV, was good for both sides. For the board it was monetary as
they were unable to continue funding the research labs, especially as medical
virology, with its attendant burgeoning costs, was a rapidly expanding field.

From the government's side a major public health concern was causing
some alarm. This was the looming threat of viral haemorrhagic fevers
and the related newly recognised formidable infectious diseases that
were appearing on the African continent. The risk of importing exotic
viral infections into the country, particularly from elsewhere in Africa,
preoccupied government minds, especially as large numbers of migrant
workers from Southern, south-eastern and Central Africa were employed
in South African mines. It was clear that there was an urgent need to
establish an institute of public health excellence in viral infections.

An agreement was reached, which saw the Department of Health purchasing the viral research component of the PRF, its site and the buildings – which would become the future NICD – for the sum of R1.3 million. The NIV duly came into being on 1 April 1976. Whoever chose that date was probably oblivious to the humorous side of that choice. While the move was necessary and timely, the shift into a government office was a serious mistake. The petty civil service rules and restrictions that came with the move greatly encumbered the functioning of the new institute. To make matters worse, South Africa had become a pariah state in the apartheid years and the accompanying international ostracism further handicapped the development of the NIV as a scientific institution.

From the Department of Health's perspective, their concerns had not been unfounded. These were quite dramatically brought to a head in early 1975 when the first recognised viral haemorrhagic fever case in South Africa was recorded.[33]

MARBURG DISEASE AND EBOLA

Marburg virus disease takes its name from the town in Germany where it was first reported in 1967. Laboratory workers in Marburg were exposed to imported monkeys from Central Africa and subsequently became infected. Characterised by a high fever (febrile) and bleeding internally and from orifices of the body (haemorrhagic), Marburg carried a high mortality. Another outbreak in 1967 was reported in Yugoslavia.

In February 1975 a young Australian traveller fell ill with an acute onset of a febrile haemorrhagic disease and died soon afterwards in the Johannesburg Hospital. He and a female companion had been hitchhiking through Zimbabwe (then Rhodesia) and Southern Africa. His companion took ill two days after the young man died. After a stormy illness, she recovered and was discharged some 40 days later. A young nursing sister who had been exposed to both patients also took ill; after a similar but somewhat milder illness, she recovered and was discharged from hospital after 21 days. Marburg virus was isolated from all three patients. Outside of Marburg, Germany, and Yugoslavia, this was the next recorded outbreak.

The viral haemorrhagic fevers, one of the dreaded new virus infections of humans, had made its appearance in Southern Africa. Population movements from countries to the north of South Africa would now pose a worrisome public health threat to South African populations. Unsurprisingly, the media contributed their fair share of alarmist reporting. Facilities for the proper nursing of patients with these formidable communicable diseases and a laboratory with the appropriate security facilities to process specimens for diagnostic and research purposes were now urgently needed. Adding further to the urgency, the following year saw calamitous outbreaks of Ebola virus haemorrhagic fever, with exceedingly high mortality rates – 88 per cent in the Congo (then Zaire) and 53 per cent in the Sudan outbreaks.[34]

Some three years later, in 1979, the Department of Health funded the construction of a maximum-security biosafety level 4 laboratory at the NIV, the only BSL-4 laboratory on the African continent.

THE NIV UNDER THE DEPARTMENT OF HEALTH (1976–1994)

The first director of the NIV was Professor O.W. (Walter/Wally) Prozesky, who also served as professor of virology at the University of Pretoria. Professor Prozesky, an internationally renowned medical virologist, played a major role in the planning and design of the NIV. He steered the fortunes of the nascent institution from April 1976 to May 1982. He also played a major role in promoting the discipline of medical virology, lobbying for and then piloting the successful registration of medical virology as an independent discipline. What was originally a relatively minor division of medical microbiology grew to become a distinctive medical speciality, recognised in 1986 as a registrable speciality by the country's regulatory authority of the time, the South African Medical and Dental Council (SAMDC) (now the Health Professions Council of South Africa, or HPCSA).

When the NIV came into being in 1976, only two universities had independent departments of virology – the University of Pretoria and the University of Stellenbosch. In other universities, virology was part of the Department of Microbiology. Medical virology was a large component of the microbiology syllabus of the undergraduate medical, dental and allied medical sciences. In 1978 the University of the Witwatersrand followed the lead of the other two universities and created an independent Department of Virology, and I was appointed as its first professor and head of that department. The intention of the establishment of a department of medical virology within the School of Pathology of the university was both to teach undergraduate and postgraduate students, as well as to provide on-site diagnostic and consultation services for the teaching hospitals – as was the case with the other medical schools in the country.

With the establishment of the NIV, the country now had a public health institution dedicated to serving as a national, regional and continental reference centre of excellence for viral diseases. In addition, the institute was responsible for producing two viral vaccines, against polio and yellow fever, and it also took on the role of teaching virology to undergraduate and postgraduate students at Wits.

On a personal note, I joined the NIV in September 1976, six months after its establishment. Walking into the post of deputy director at the age of 31 presented me with a number of significant challenges. The team of scientific and medical personnel inherited by the NIV had been with the PRF for decades, and they were clearly not exactly enamoured with having to now report to a young outsider. The PRF community were a close-knit team of scientific and medical personnel, medical technologists, and also auxiliary workers responsible for vaccine production. The last mentioned consisted of women who lived in the vicinity of the institute and who were meticulous, thorough and dedicated to vaccine production. As the institute was situated adjacent to a residential area called Sandringham, this army of female workers became known as 'the Sandringham housewives'. The remoulding of the organisation into a modern diagnostic and research laboratory required a great deal of tact, patience and sensitivity.

Shortly after the birth of the NIV, thoughts turned to constructing facilities to work with the most formidable and dangerous viral pathogens – which had, of course, been one of the foremost reasons for establishing the NIV. Fortunately, help came in the form of the same engineers who had been responsible for the construction of the maximum-security laboratories, the BSL-4 laboratories, of the CDC. The NIV's BSL-4 laboratory began functioning in 1979.

Under the stewardship of Wally Prozesky, the NIV became a leading virological institute on the global map and served as the reference centre of expertise for much of the African continent. Prozesky was instrumental in establishing valuable international contacts, especially with the CDC, the pre-eminent public health institution of the US. He resigned from the NIV in 1982 to take up the post of vice-rector of the University of Pretoria and, later on, president of the MRC.

In June 1982, I was appointed director of the NIV. In the latter part of the 1980s, the decision was taken to cease vaccine production, which had become uneconomical, especially with the increasingly sophisticated safety testing requirements. At the same time the low cost of purchasing imported polio vaccine made local production financially imprudent.

Moving into the latter part of the twentieth century, the NIV became the major medical virological reference training and research institute for the African continent and served as a reference centre for the WHO for a number of viral diseases. The staff complement had tripled, and the institute was able to attract a great number of well-qualified and productive scientists to its ranks. However, two serious challenges hampered the progress of the NIV. These were political interference and international ostracism.

The political clouds

Fear played a significant role in the purchase of the PRF laboratories by the apartheid government of the day to establish the NIV. In the mid 1970s South Africa was already a global pariah state, and the boycotts and the isolation of the country were starting to bite. This was becoming a real concern to the academic and scientific community. The government mandated that South Africa needed to become more independent of the outside world and as self-sufficient as possible. This should extend, so the authorities believed, to medicines and vaccines. A well-functioning, scientifically grounded and productive institute for diagnosis and research into viral diseases, which could also ensure the country's needs for at least some viral vaccines, was an important part of becoming self-sufficient.

Furthermore, a facility with expertise and resources for the early diagnosis of and rapid response to exotic viral diseases was sorely needed. The threat of importation of these formidable diseases was growing with the ever-increasing work-seeking population from countries to the north, where many of these diseases were largely uncontrolled. Indeed, the Marburg virus incident of 1975 was a timely wake-up call and provided proof, if any were needed, of the urgency for having such an institute.

An additional cogent motivation, or at least perceived to be so by the government, was the menace of biological warfare. South Africa was at war with the African liberation armies in Namibia and Angola to the north-west of the country, which were augmented by Cuban and East German expeditionary forces. The engine of communist paranoia was a powerful one and the spectre of biological warfare was taken very seriously. In fact South Africa had secretly developed its own biological and chemical warfare programme.[35] The retention of stocks of smallpox virus at the NIV in the face of urgent appeals by the WHO and the international scientific community to destroy these last remaining stocks of the virus stored in the institute's fridges was prompted by paranoid fears of biological warfare.

With this background, there was plainly no way that the infant NIV could be allowed free rein. The political need to keep tight control on the institute would soon put a restraint on its ability to fully develop its potential as a scientific centre of excellence. The lodestone of the combined burdens of bureaucracy and political interference weighed heavily on the NIV, both during its tenure under the apartheid government until 1994, and also when it fell under the control of the new democratic government from 1994 to 2000. The bureaucratic restraints were less evident between 1976 and 1982, but as time moved on, the woes of the NIV only increased.

Hierarchies, rules and regulations

The NIV, as a reference centre of excellence for virus diseases on the southern tip of the African continent, indisputably fulfilled an urgent public health need nationally, regionally and globally. However, it did not take long for the realisation to set in that a cardinal mistake had been made in positioning the NIV to be an office of the Department of Health and still expect the institute to realise its potential to deliver satisfactorily on its mandate.

The Department of Health was housed in an imposing 27-storey building called Civitas, which prominently outlines the skyline of the northern reaches of metropolitan Pretoria. It was entrusted with implementing the government's health strategy and national responsibilities, which included preventive health and health education. The delivery of curative healthcare through public hospitals and health clinics was, and still remains, the remit of the respective health departments of the nine provinces of the country and the local authorities of the larger metropoles.

The hierarchical organisation of the Department of Health at the time was made up of the director general (DG) of health, who reported directly to the minister of health. Under the DG were the deputy director generals (DDGs), and reporting to the DDGs were the various chief directorates. The NIV was pigeonholed into a sub-programme called Laboratory Services within the chief directorate of forensic services. Dr Colin Cameron, a veterinarian, and Dr Pieter Aucamp, an environmental scientist, served, in turn, as the chief directors, and within their responsibilities lay the governance of the NIV until 1994. The last minister of health in the apartheid government was a social worker, Dr Rina Venter, who, incidentally, was the first woman cabinet minister in the history of South Africa.

The bureaucratic yoke

The day-to-day running of the NIV now needed to comply with the rules and regulations that pertained to all the government departments of the day. The administrative routine and the rigid, unyielding requirements of governmental civil service may have been well suited to the offices of the Civitas warren of the Department of Health, but not so for the NIV. Unsurprisingly, frustration built and clashes between Civitas and the NIV were not long in coming.

It is well known that the satisfactory management of human resources is key to the success of any organisation. This applied even more so to the NIV, which was competing with academia and the pharmaceutical industry to attract and retain suitably qualified scientific professionals and support staff from a very limited pool of specialist personnel. The Department of Health obstructionism came soon and was not in short supply.

An example of their diktats related to the process to be followed when a post became vacant. In the NIV context, a vacant post remained open until a suitable professional could be found. In the Department of Health context, however, if it wasn't filled a vacant post would be precariously under threat of being abolished, unless a strong motivating story was composed to convince the relevant official at Civitas of its indispensable need.

Another example can be found in the system of reward. An employee of the institute deserving of a promotion or bonus, whether a clerical assistant or a senior scientist, required supporting 'incidents' to be composed to accompany the application. The motivation required evidence in writing for each of three designated qualities: responsibility, insight and productivity. It is ludicrous looking back on it now, but at the time it could be depressingly frustrating. Exemplars of 'incidents' (some with accompanying illustrations) were kindly provided by the department. Essentially they were relevant to a hospital environment.

These kinds of narratives, clearly a measure of literary skill more than vocational merit, were expected by the then Department of Health from all its employees, office cleaners and senior scientists alike, in support of reward or promotion. Suitable compositions were required to accompany applications. Numerous examples are on record of applications to motivate good performance from the relevant supervisors of employees of the NIV being flatly turned down by officials of the department simply on the grounds of 'inadequate incidentation' [*sic*].

There was also much focus on discipline. In my capacity as director I was regularly summoned to be present at meetings of the executive of the Department of Health in Pretoria. These were generally very lengthy meetings, for the most part discussing administrative and managerial matters. Non-attendance, however, evoked stern rebuke, along the lines of: 'Please provide urgently an explanation for this behaviour to be submitted to the Director General who is personally the chairman of the meeting.'[36]

The burden of the political

There is no question that the activities of the NIV crossed on occasion into delicate, tricky and, at times, even precarious sensitivities during the apartheid years, especially in its relationship with a media hungry for sensation. Civitas was very well aware of the potential minefield of the media and appropriately tight controls were put in place on the NIV. As the national reference centre for viral diseases, the NIV was frequently called on by the media to provide expert opinion and comment to the public on virological issues and incidents involving virus infection.

Added to the contrast between the professional staff of the NIV and the officialdom of the Department of Health, the degree of trust in matters of communication on scientific questions with the outside world was low. Written permission had to be received from Civitas before the NIV director could be interviewed in any form on radio, television or in print. Permission would usually be forthcoming, but virtually always with strings and conditions attached. For example, when a request was received at the institute for a radio or TV interview, permission was granted only if the questions to be asked at the interview were sent beforehand to the director and then forwarded to be scrutinised for approval by the department in Pretoria. (Sometimes the questions were simply fabricated at the NIV and often came to bear no semblance to what was actually discussed in the interview.) As a humorous example, during my term as director a request in 1991 came to the NIV for me to appear on a radio show called 'Sex Talk' to discuss AIDS and other sexually transmitted diseases. The approval letter came with the condition that one of the Department of Health officials (a general practitioner) accompany me to 'handle the clinical side' of the interview.[37] Another example, in January 1990, for permission for an interview on bedbugs for a commercial magazine came with the comment from the chief director in Civitas 'to ensure that the article is not sensational and that no official authority is unduly criticised'.[38]

Even submissions from senior NIV staff for scientific publications came with conditions such as 'approved subject to minor adjustments' – adjustments made by the veterinary-qualified chief director. When it came to the very touchy subject of HIV/AIDS, permission needed to come not from the Department of Health but from the DG of foreign affairs.

The apex of bureaucratic horrors belonged to the minefield for applications to attend scientific conferences abroad. The guidelines for applications for permission for overseas trips ran into two foolscap typed pages of instructions. Applications, inter alia, required strong motivation and had to be submitted well in advance to the executive of the Department of Health for their consideration, before being submitted to the minister for final approval. Many a time applications were refused simply because the motivations did not meet the administrative minutiae demanded by Civitas. More often than not there would be no financial implications for the institute or the Department of Health, as these trips would be by invitation from organisations such as the WHO, or would be funded by grants from a research organisation. On occasion, successful travel grants awarded by research-funding organisations such as the PRF would be rejected by the Department of Health and would have to be refunded.

Desperate times

As early as a year after I was appointed director of the NIV, I sent a strongly worded appeal for help to the then DG of health, Professor François Retief. Some nine years later a similar desperate plea was addressed to the next DG of health, Professor Coen Slabber. Both DGs were previously deans of medical schools, and both were urbane, distinguished senior academics. Unfortunately, academic-to-academic entreaties were also of no avail. The bureaucratic mountain was simply too high. After visiting the NIV, both distinguished academics followed up with very polite and encouraging letters, but unfortunately, all their good reassurances were simply quashed once the lower levels of the department became involved. Nothing transpired.

Appeals were sent to the chairman of the board of the PRF as well as the dean of the medical school of the University of the Witwatersrand. Meetings were held but no movement to try to improve the situation could be discerned. Approaches were then made to move the NIV from the Department of Health and to look at relocating it to the MRC, then headed by Professor Wally Prozesky. While this move would have given the institute more autonomy, the essential role of the NIV as a public health institute and a diagnostic and vaccine production facility did not fit comfortably into the remit of the MRC. The Department of Health undertook an investigation to look at possibly revising the reporting structure of the NIV with the aim of allowing the institute greater man-agement autonomy. However, the senior management of the Department of Health decided to retain the status quo.

In despair, I responded to the department in March 1990:

> Further to my previous letters I must again reiterate my pro-
> found despondency, not only concerning the prognosis for the
> Institute in general but also, in my own personal situation, my
> particular resentment at the inordinate amount of inroads into
> my professional functioning as an academic and consultant
> virologist, that the often futile administrative bureaucracy is
> accounting for.[39]

A year later, just before I went on sabbatical leave, I included the following
in a letter to the DDG of the Department of Health:

> Further to our discussions after the PRF board meeting on Saturday,
> 30 November, I do think you will appreciate that I will not be able
> to continue as Director of the NIV under the conditions where the
> NIV is managed as an administrative office rather than as a scien-
> tific institution.[40]

There is no doubt that much damage was done to the potential of the
NIV as a centre of excellence and the value it could have provided to the
nation. Perhaps it was the six-month absence from the institute which
allowed me to reconsider my resignation, because I decided to return
after my sabbatical and persevere. On quiet reflection during this six-
month period, I came to realise what an incredible team of dedicated
scientists and support personnel made up the institute. As director
I could not have wished for a more loyal and devoted crew on board the
NIV. It was an institute with a very special mission and the women and
men who drove the ship were more than up to the task. It was this very
special family that salvaged the institution. One can but hope that the
serious mistake of trying to manage a public health institution within the
bureaucratic entanglement of government is not repeated in the future.

Notwithstanding all the obstacles, the NIV did grow and develop, and it made a major contribution to national and international public health. However, there was one more serious handicap to contend with, an obstacle imposed on the institute from outside – international isolation.

International ostracism

The gathering clouds of international condemnation of the apartheid government's internal policies did not leave the NIV untouched. The academic boycott of South Africa in the early 1980s significantly compromised research collaboration with the outside world. By then, international funding for research had virtually dried up. While I personally was privileged to benefit from a US postdoctoral research fellowship in 1977, at the final debriefing before I left the US to come home, I was reminded by the US authorities that I was the last recipient of that award. This situation would persist until the advent of the democratic government in 1994.

Colleagues with whom we enjoyed warm and often personal relationships found themselves unable to come out to a country saddled with the blight of apartheid. Peter Piot, one of the most prominent senior international researchers in the fields of viral haemorrhagic fevers and HIV/AIDS (later to become the director of the London School of Hygiene and Tropical Medicine), wrote to me on 25 November 1987:

> Dear Barry, Thank you for your letter of 29 October 1987 and your kind invitation. I am sorry to let you know that I've decided not to visit South Africa for the time being, since I feel increasingly uncomfortable with the politics of apartheid. This has nothing to do with my personal feelings for the many friends I have in your country, as I know that most of you are also not happy with the current situation.[41]

Similarly, a letter dated 17 December 1987 from the late Geoffrey Rose of the London School of Hygiene and Tropical Medicine:

> It gives me extreme distress to take this position [of turning down the NIV invitation] because between ourselves as medical scientists all my desire is for close collaboration and mutual support. Such a decision is neither clear-cut nor easy and I wish with all my heart I did not feel bound to make it, but you will perhaps understand why I feel driven to such a position. It has seemed to me to be impossible to visit South Africa without some participation in and subjection to the apartheid system.[42]

Participation in international projects and collaboration with international colleagues was eventually all but sealed off. Very few international contacts remained, tenuously grasped by our scientists with their fingernails. Through some indirect channels, the NIV managed to hold on to a few international fora. Dr James Gilliland, a former DDG of health and former vice-chair of the board of the PRF, was also a senior office-holder in Rotary International. Through the goodwill of Gilliland's Rotary connections, the NIV managed to keep its place as a surveillance laboratory for the WHO influenza surveillance programme.

Despite all these constraints, the NIV nevertheless managed to survive the severe blow of international ostracism, and, somehow, it even managed to grow.

3

Putting together the National Institute for Communicable Diseases

One of the earliest priorities of the new government of the country in 1994 was to remedy the past inequalities of healthcare delivery and also to provide much-needed institutional support for public health. The idea to create a national public health institution specifically for communicable diseases, which accounted for some 70 per cent of the health burden of sub-Saharan Africa, was first raised in 1995. Some six years later it was the establishment of the more broadly encompassing NHLS which finally enabled the creation of the NICD, in 2001. Again, meddlesome, unproductive political interference threw obstacles onto the pathway of its development.

The proposed new national health plan was contained in a document entitled 'A National Health Plan for South Africa' and was published in May 1994. The document set out a comprehensive health programme with the express goal of providing health benefits to all South Africans.[43] The elements of the plan were directed at strengthening health systems over a broad spectrum of healthcare. In particular, there was a focus on redressing the past inequities of health delivery. This included the building of capacity in the health sector and improving the effectiveness and efficiency of all components of the health system for all sectors of the population. Laboratory services were singled out as being one component of healthcare delivery that needed to be remedied, as it was 'plagued by gross fragmentation and duplication with serious disparities in laboratory service provision, especially along racial and geographic lines'.[44] Not surprisingly, the national health plan included a section on laboratory services and called for the establishment of a national health laboratory service.

THE NATIONAL HEALTH LABORATORY SERVICE (NHLS)

Soon after April 1994, the newly appointed minister of health, Dr Nkosazana Zuma, appointed a task team under the chairmanship of Professor Jan van den Ende, previously director of the SAIMR and head of medical microbiology at the universities of the Free State and Natal, to address the challenge of establishing an effective and comprehensive national laboratory service for the country. The team was tasked with creating a plan to consolidate all public-sector medical laboratories. Following the release of the Van den Ende report, a project implementation team was created to put into effect the restructuring of the public health laboratory services of the country.

Laboratory services responsible for the public health sector were provided from three sources. Firstly, the SAIMR was responsible for the lion's share and, although headquartered in Johannesburg, it owned and managed laboratories throughout the country. Secondly, provincial laboratories were present in the larger provinces and were owned and managed by their respective provincial departments of health. Thirdly, the eight medical schools provided laboratory services to their respective teaching hospitals.

The project implementation team was tasked with consolidating this motley collection of disparate laboratories and management structures into one organisation. The consolidated national laboratory service was initially called Healthlab Africa but was later named the National Health Laboratory Service (NHLS). The laboratories of eight of the nine provinces joined immediately; the remaining one, KwaZulu-Natal, came in after a few years.

The laboratories constituting the NHLS ranged from entities as simple as a depot to receive and transmit specimens, to small peripheral laboratories with limited functions, through to the highly specialised reference laboratories in the academic centres. Special arrangements were made with the universities to provide for academic activities in addition to the routine laboratory service requirements. The combination of diagnostic laboratory services with academic teaching responsibilities came to be known as the hybrid model.

The leader of the project appointed in 1999 was Dr Nicholas Crisp, previously the head of provincial health for Limpopo Province. Months of hard work culminated with the publication of the National Health Laboratory Service Act No. 37 of 2000 in December 2000. The proclamation signed by the president determined 1 October 2001 to be the date that the NHLS became the legally responsible authority for all laboratory services for the public health sector in South Africa.

PUBLIC HEALTH INSTITUTIONS

The term 'public health' has been variously defined. In essence, the concept of 'public health' is generally understood to be those elements of health systems that are distinct from those of curative medical services, which are aimed at healthcare delivery to individual patients. The preventive-oriented public health component forms a relatively small part of a health system compared to the delivery of curative individual-level health services. Nevertheless, its contribution is a crucial cog in the effective machinery of the health systems of a country.

In practice, the science of public health is a composite of a number of disciplines whose goal is to improve the health outcomes of the population of countries. Prevention of ill health spans communicable and non-communicable diseases, environmental hazards, natural and man-made disasters, and behavioural and lifestyle practices promoting health and preventing disease.

Dedicated public health institutions have been established throughout the world. The International Association of National Public Health Institutes (IANPHI) was established in 2006 with 39 founding members. It has grown, as of 20 November 2022, to 115 members in 98 countries.[45] The NICD of South Africa was one of the earliest members and also served on the board of IANPHI.

Foremost among the activities of a public health institution is the provision of scientific evidence to guide the health policies of the government and to design safe and effective interventions to address potential health threats and promote the healthy well-being of the country's citizens.[46] Scientifically established data on disease burdens, including statistics on the prevalence or spread of diseases, their geographic locations, risk factors and a host of other determinants of disease, all fall under the rubric 'epidemiology' – probably one of the most frequently used terms in public health medical science.

The NICD as a public health institute

The urgency for establishing a public health institute to address communicable diseases was underlined by the reality that communicable diseases are responsible for some 70 per cent of the burden of ill health in sub-Saharan Africa.[47] The effective management of communicable diseases was widely recognised to be a particularly urgent public health challenge to the health system of South Africa.[48]

The idea to establish a public health institute for communicable diseases came to light on 23 November 1995. On that day, I penned a letter to the then DG and the DDG of health. The submission pointed out that there was an urgent need to establish a public health institute in South Africa which would serve as a centre of excellence and reference centre for communicable diseases, and be a facility with the necessary expertise to respond rapidly to emergencies and public health threats from infectious diseases. This institution could play an invaluable role in supporting efforts to control communicable diseases in South Africa and also regionally and, indeed, the whole continent. It could represent South Africa and the region at the various international bodies, such as WHO and the CDC, concerned with global health.

Furthermore, two institutions involved with communicable diseases already existed in South Africa which, if simply moulded together, could form the building blocks of a communicable disease institution. The two were the microbiology and entomology laboratories of the SAIMR on the one hand, and the virology laboratories of the NIV on the other. The geographical siting of the NIV was a further attraction. The NIV was located on a large tract of land in the suburb of Rietfontein in north-east Johannesburg, about 15 minutes away from O.R. Tambo International Airport, the gateway to the country and, to a large extent, much of the continent.

While the seed of the NICD was thus planted in 1995, it took another four years for it to germinate in 1999, and a further three years for it to fully flower on 1 April 2002, when the microbiology laboratories functionally joined the virology arm from the NIV under one management.

At that stage, the microbiology and entomology laboratories were still geographically situated within the SAIMR's central site in downtown Johannesburg, some 12 kilometres from the virology laboratories on the Rietfontein site. It took a further three years for those laboratories physically to be moved to Rietfontein and to be housed within a large building on the site which previously had housed the bacterial vaccine production plant of the South African Vaccine Producers (SAVP). With the closing down of that plant, this building became available for the microbiology laboratories. The third component of the proposal was to create, de novo, an epidemiological unit for surveillance and data management.

Nurtured by its parent organisations – the NIV and the SAIMR – the infant NICD grew rapidly. It wasn't long before it took its place as the country's centre of excellence for communicable diseases and became an African reference centre on the global health stage.

The obstacles

The idea seemed good, and the preparations had been thorough and robust, but the pathway to the establishment of the NICD was not all plain sailing. At the end of 1995, the idea remained just that – an attractive proposal which, at least, warranted serious consideration. What eventually allowed the idea to become a reality was a process taking shape at the same time in a wider sphere. This was the restructuring of the public health laboratories of the country as mentioned above under the developing NHLS within the wider national health plan.

The embryo of the NICD nestled within the developing NHLS and at last was seriously starting to take shape along the lines of the original proposal. Integral to the proposal was that the new institute should be a truly national organisation.

A particularly sensitive issue, from the earliest stages, was the proposal to locate the new institute on the Rietfontein site on the border of Johannesburg within a relatively short distance from only one of the eight university medical schools of the country, namely, Wits. Until this time, the academic responsibilities for that university were supplied both by the SAIMR and the NIV, the parent organisations of the NICD, through its School of Pathology. Would that university now be the sole or main beneficiary of the new proposal?

An additional sensitivity was that some of the proposed functions for the new institute were already ostensibly being carried out by existing bodies, especially research and data-handling functions under the aegis of the MRC. An extensive country-wide tour became necessary to smooth things over and provide the reassurances of mutual benefit to organisations throughout the country.

In the main, the proposal to establish a national institute for communicable diseases was endorsed and received widespread support. Approval was not universal, however. As was the case with the efforts of my esteemed mentor Professor James Gear a half-century previously concerning polio vaccination, so did the creation of the NICD meet with hurdles and obstacles along the way. Marie Curie could not have said it better: 'I was taught that the way of progress was neither swift nor easy.' No sooner had the obstacle of academic affiliation been addressed than a new bogey reared its head – this time it was the political bogey.

In 1999 the country had only recently emerged from its apartheid past, and trust and co-operation were still evolving and being consolidated. Elements in the new Department of Health were suspicious and highly critical of the plans. To illustrate the depth of animus, I was the recipient of a most distasteful, hostile and personally offensive letter. It came from a very high-level and influential quarter and read in part as follows:

> More unethical is the fact that this document is prepared by individual/s with vested interests, little or no experience of such a structure and thus conflicts of interest in this issue . . .
>
> It is regrettable that those who benefitted from apartheid are today becoming experts to rewrite or re-engineer themselves and us. The document is the dream of one individual and not a collective that has the national interest at heart. I find this totally unacceptable.[49]

At this low point in the development of the NICD, there were nevertheless a number of encouraging voices who provided valuable support. Among these voices was an indomitable individual who played an important role in smoothing over these early difficulties and contributed greatly to the early development of the institute – Professor Salim Abdool Karim. Professor Abdool Karim and his renowned research partner and wife, Quarraisha, were among South Africa's leading scientists in the field of understanding epidemiology, the prevention of HIV in particular, and infectious diseases in general. Later, during the Covid-19 pandemic, Professor Abdool Karim served as the country's most senior adviser in the management of that epidemic. His contributions to the science of infectious diseases have been recognised globally in that he has been honoured with some of the most prestigious international awards.

Overcoming these birth pains, the NICD came into being as a division of the NHLS, together with the birth of the latter in 2001. The formal integration of the microbiology, parasitology and entomology laboratories of the former SAIMR to constitute the NICD was made official on 1 April 2002 – exactly 26 years after the formation of the NIV from its predecessor PRF laboratories.

The NICD – its mission

The mission statement employed to lobby for the establishment of the NICD read: 'The NICD will be a resource of knowledge and expertise in regionally relevant communicable diseases, in order to assist in the planning of policies and programmes and to support appropriate responses to communicable disease problems and issues.'

Eight objectives were formulated for the future institute:

1. To be a national organ for public health surveillance of communicable diseases.
2. To collect, analyse and interpret communicable disease data on an ongoing and systematic basis.
3. To continuously and systematically monitor for the emergence of new communicable diseases, for the re-emergence or re-appearance of previously controlled communicable diseases, and the importation of exotic communicable diseases.
4. To detect outbreaks or epidemics at an early stage, in order to be able to timeously and effectively respond to them, or to anticipate imminent outbreaks or epidemics by investigation, research and analysis of data.
5. To engage in directed and relevant research to answer questions related to regional public health communicable disease problems and their surveillance and management.

6. To establish formal structures for the rapid and continuous dissemination of data and information generated from NICD to all who need to know.
7. To build capacity in communicable diseases nationally and regionally.
8. To provide a reference function to communicable disease laboratories in the public and private sectors nationally and regionally.

The goals set out for the newborn institute with its 300-strong personnel were indeed ambitious, if not fearfully daunting. Three divisions were formed: a virology division, formed from the predecessor NIV; a microbiology division comprised of the bacteriology, parasitology and entomology laboratories of the predecessor SAIMR; and a tiny embryonic epidemiology and surveillance unit.

The laboratories from the SAIMR were only physically relocated several months after the birth of the NICD in 2005, while appropriate renovations and alterations were completed in the SAVP building. At a later stage, in 2011, under the second director of the NICD, Professor Shabir Madhi, the structure was further reorganised into what are currently called centres, based on their respective disease responsibilities.

Currently, the NICD has seven of these centres: the Centre for Emerging Zoonotic and Parasitic Diseases; the Centre for Enteric Diseases; the Centre for Healthcare-Associated Infections, Antimicrobial Resistance and Mycoses; the Centre for HIV and STIs (sexually transmitted infections); the Centre for Respiratory Diseases and Meningitis; the Centre for Tuberculosis; and the Centre for Vaccines and Immunology.

4

Surveillance of communicable diseases

Professionals in the medical field understand quite clearly what is meant by the terms 'epidemiology' and 'surveillance', but usually have difficulty in defining them. Practically speaking, these two terms can be usefully employed to describe the role of the NICD to provide data and information on the status of communicable diseases in the country. This is the bread-and-butter occupation of a public health institution like the NICD. Its activities cover the wide array of infectious agents: viral, bacterial, fungal and parasitic. This information and data are crucial for guiding public health authorities, nationally and internationally, and informing both the medical profession and the general public.

Some 60 years ago Alexander D. Langmuir, widely regarded as the father of modern communicable diseases surveillance and epidemiology, defined what is encompassed by the discipline of disease surveillance:

> Surveillance, when applied to disease, means the continued watchfulness over the distribution and trends of incidence through the systematic collection, consolidation and evaluation of morbidity

and mortality reports and other relevant data. Intrinsic in the concept is the regular dissemination of the basic data and interpretations to all who have contributed and to all others who need to know. The concept, however, does not encompass direct responsibility for control activities. These traditionally have been and still remain with the state and local health authorities.[50]

More recently, the pandemic of Covid-19, the ongoing threat of viral haemorrhagic fevers and the burden of HIV/AIDS and TB have underlined the critical value of a well-run, scientifically informed surveillance programme.[51] The success of communicable diseases surveillance, as is the case with surveillance for exposure to noxious chemicals, is crucially dependent on the timeliness of being alerted to the earliest signals of an impending outbreak. For example, surveillance of wastewater to detect the circulation of pathogenic organisms,[52] such as SARS-CoV-2, or surveillance of acute flaccid paralysis (AFP) (the typical clinical sign of polio),[53] have been shown to be effective tools for the early detection of impending outbreaks. Prompt responses to effect control measures need to be initiated as early as possible before an outbreak erupts in a population.

Surveillance instruments are multiple and varied. The design of a surveillance resource or source of a sentinel specimen is determined by how easily available and practical a resource is, and how likely it is to provide timely information.

Communicable disease surveillance programmes are, of course, considerably broader than only for the purpose of early detection. So, for example, monitoring the efficacy of interventions employed to control outbreaks provides important information to policymakers to guide decisions on the most effective interventions for reducing the impact of outbreaks.

Outbreaks may be of the high-prevalence but low-mortality variety, such as the common respiratory epidemics like influenza, where transmission of the organism is facilitated by widespread human-to-human contact, or localised and circumscribed, such as foodborne or water-borne outbreaks of diarrhoeal disease. Alternatively, they may be low-prevalence high-mortality outbreaks, as seen with a number of zoonotic (coming from animals) infections. With these outbreaks, alertness and vigilance are particularly important for the early detection of warning signals of impending threats – for example, in the case of viral haemor-rhagic fevers.

COMMUNICABLE DISEASES SURVEILLANCE AT THE NICD

Not surprisingly, given its public health mantle, surveillance and monitoring of communicable diseases and providing data to author-ities was one of the earliest priorities of the NICD's three predecessor institutions, the SAIMR, the PRF and the NIV, and subsequently, the NICD.

In the years following the 1994 democratisation of South Africa, and the entry of the NIV and the SAIMR into the global scientific commu-nity, their role as critical resources for the rapid and timely monitoring of communicable diseases became increasingly important and their respon-sibility nationally, regionally and for the continent was widely recognised and supported. Before long, international bodies such as the WHO recognised the crucial importance of the NICD as a laboratory resource, as a sentinel for communicable diseases regionally and the African con-tinent, and, in addition, as a training centre. With political barriers now removed, the WHO accorded Regional Reference Laboratory and Collaborating Centre status to the NICD for a full spectrum of commu-nicable diseases (see Appendix 2), thus enabling the NICD to become a major partner in the global public health arena for the monitoring of communicable diseases.

To carry out this mandate of surveillance and detection of early signs of impending outbreaks, as well as managing the effectiveness of responses to control them, an autonomous Division of Public Health Surveillance and Response was created which traversed several of the laboratory programmes. Its role was to co-ordinate information coming from a wide spectrum of the laboratory activities of the institute. Supplementary laboratory data were also fed in from the network of public and private laboratories throughout the country.

The following are some examples of the public health surveillance activities of the NICD.

Influenza surveillance

The first toe-in-the-water venture into a formal surveillance programme at the NIV focused on the most regular and most common seasonal illness that we all experience – influenza or, more broadly, acute respiratory illness, at a primary healthcare level. Established in 1984, the fledgling Viral Watch Programme developed into an extensive and comprehensive surveillance and monitoring programme for all communicable diseases and positioned the future NICD to be a regional sentinel facility and a crucial component of the WHO's global monitoring programme of communicable diseases.[54]

Initially, the programme started with some 15 to 20 sentinel doctors who came from a variety of monitoring centres – private general practitioners, primary healthcare centre doctors, mineworker health facilities, and clinics in paediatric and adult hospitals. Data on illnesses at the primary healthcare level were actively recruited from these healthcare professionals. The information was supplemented with passive surveillance data from the routine specimens which were sent to the diagnostic laboratories of the institute. The portrait of influenza was charted annually from the laboratory data and clinical data supplied by the sentinel doctors. The Viral Watch was also supplemented with feedback on the extent of illness affecting children through a school absenteeism surveillance programme which monitored some 8 000 primary and high school children.

Focusing predominantly on respiratory illness, useful trends could be demonstrated showing the cyclical regularity of respiratory illness in the winter season but varying in severity from year to year with specific strains of influenza being associated with outbreaks of greater or lesser severity.

Participating doctors were provided with collection material to submit specimens for laboratory diagnosis of their patients' illnesses. This was, of course, also of great value to practitioners, who were empowered with the knowledge of what was 'going around' at any particular time. A monthly publication, the *South African Virus Laboratories Surveillance Bulletin*, was established at the NIV, which published data and editorials from the surveillance programme. This was supplemented with contributions from all the academic virology laboratories in medical schools throughout the country and was widely distributed to doctors and public health authorities.

The Viral Watch Programme also played an important role in global health. In addition to supplying clinical data for a particular strain circulating in the southern hemisphere winter season, the programme also contributed to identifying new strains of influenza viruses. The influenza laboratory became the first designated WHO collaborating laboratory of the NIV and survived even the lean years when the South African scientific community suffered international ostracism.

The laboratory surveillance of the influenza viruses obtained from the Viral Watch Programme plays an important role in the WHO's global influenza virus surveillance programme, informing global authorities which strains are circulating in the human population at a particular time – generally in the winter season.[55] Influenza viruses isolated from these sentinel sources are characterised in the laboratory and typed using panels of standardised serum reagents provided by the WHO, in addition to the genetic sequencing of the virus isolates. An important characteristic of influenza viruses is that they are genetically and antigenically unstable. ('Antigen' denotes the protein structure of the organism which is recognised by the immune system of the body following an infection or following vaccination. It is the target of the protective immune response.) Because of this, for vaccines to be effective in combating influenza, they need to be updated every year to match the prevalent strain of virus circulating in the population.

Twice a year virologists from around the world meet at the WHO headquarters in Geneva to make recommendations on selecting the most ideal strains of the influenza virus to constitute the influenza vaccine for the forthcoming season. Isolates from laboratories worldwide are typed and then sent to a handful of specialist collaborating laboratories around the world for confirmation. Strains that have genetically drifted to take on a new specific antigenic identity are then labelled with their laboratory of origin and the year of isolation. These isolates are sent on to the vaccine manufacturers to be incorporated into the forthcoming vaccine. In 1994 one of the strains used for the influenza vaccine originated in the NIV – A/Johannesburg/33/94(H3N2).

In February the WHO meeting plans for the northern hemisphere winter season, and in September for the southern hemisphere winter season. The closer the strains incorporated into the vaccine match up with what is circulating in the population, the more effective the vaccine turns out to be.

This information, together with the actual isolates of the virus, is passed on to vaccine manufacturers to manufacture the influenza vaccines for the coming winter influenza season. In some years the match is good; in others, the virus has gained the upper hand with a more abrupt change, termed 'antigenic drift'. The experience of influenza in the winter of the relatively few southern hemisphere countries is of particular importance to the more populous northern hemisphere in planning their vaccine composition. In this regard, the NIV/NICD sentinel laboratory plays a particularly valuable global surveillance role.

GERMS-SA

Another early surveillance programme, which has the quaintly appropriate acronym GERMS-SA (South African Group for Enteric Respiratory and Meningeal Diseases), was established to co-ordinate data on bacterial infections from some 200 microbiology laboratories throughout the country.

One of the very prominent outbreaks diagnosed and investigated by the enteric bacterial laboratory in the GERMS-SA programme was the listeriosis epidemic of 2017/2018, which was also the largest outbreak of this organism ever recorded.[56] This foodborne severe gastroenteritis is caused by bacteria of the genus *Listeria*. Over 1 000 cases were diagnosed in the laboratory, and the outbreak resulted in 216 deaths. The investigation was facilitated by the employment of advanced instrumentation (the next-generation whole genome sequencer), which, as the name implies, has the capacity to sequence the entire genome of the organism. The source of the infection was traced to contaminated ready-to-eat processed meat products.

The economic impact of the outbreak was immense. Immediately following the announcement of the cause of the outbreak, the stock price of the company Tiger Brands, one of South Africa's major food producers, fell by seven per cent on the Johannesburg Stock Exchange – a loss of some R5.7 billion, at the time equivalent to US$438.69 million. A class action lawsuit against the company by 1 000 claimants is still pending.[57]

Antimicrobial resistance surveillance

The widespread use, overuse and misuse of antibiotics in hospitals, in clinics and even in animal feeds has resulted in one of the most urgent and serious threats to public health – namely, antimicrobial resistance. The extent and implications of the twenty-first-century global crisis of drug-resistant infections are often under-appreciated. A 2016 review of antimicrobial resistance estimated that some 700 000 people die annually as a result of drug resistance.[58] There is clearly an urgent need to respond resolutely to stem the progress of this serious threat to public health.

Former UK Prime Minister David Cameron articulated the extent of the crisis in 2014, when he said: 'If we fail to act, we are looking at an almost unthinkable scenario, where antibiotics no longer work, and we are cast back into the dark ages of medicine.'[59]

Inappropriate use of antibiotics and other antimicrobial agents sets the scene for multiplying organisms to be readily selected for their ability to develop resistance to antibiotics, antifungal agents, antiviral agents and even insecticides used to control anopheline mosquitoes (the carriers of malaria). As early as 1945, the discoverer of penicillin, Sir Alexander Fleming, warned of the danger of wholesale antibiotic overuse leading to organisms becoming resistant.

Today, there are micro-organisms, often in the hospital environment and including common infectious agents, that have developed resistance to virtually all antibiotics. This is further aggravated by the commercial disincentive for manufacturers to invest in research for the development of new antibiotics or other antibacterial agents. Over the past four decades, the repertoire of available antimicrobial agents has yielded only a handful of novel alternatives to existing antibiotics.[60]

The antimicrobial resistance reference laboratory of the NICD was established to provide a diagnostic and reference centre for bacterial and fungal resistance, including a facility for molecular genetic studies, to further investigate and characterise the mechanisms of the resistance. To gain some idea of the severity of antimicrobial resistance, one needs only to look at two common bacteria which were initially easily treated with the earliest of antibiotics – penicillin.

The pneumococcus, an important cause of pneumonia, meningitis and other clinical syndromes, has rapidly developed resistance not only to penicillin but to a wide range of new antibiotics, greatly complicating the treatment of this infective agent.[61] Similarly, gonococcus, the cause of gonorrhoea, which was highly sensitive to penicillin and other antibiotics, has now become highly resistant to nearly all antibiotics.[62] The WHO has established an international surveillance programme to monitor gonococcal resistance, not inappropriately called GASP (Gonococcal Antimicrobial Surveillance Programme).

Tuberculosis (TB)

TB rarely features prominently in the media spotlight in South Africa, and yet South Africa is home to one of the highest incidences of the disease in the world.[63] During the era of the Covid-19 pandemic, TB ranked second only to Covid as a cause of death due to a communicable agent. The WHO report of 2021 estimated around 328 000 cases of the disease in South Africa, with 61 000 deaths, 36 000 of which were accompanied by HIV.[64]

The Centre for TB of the NICD is housed in its own, purpose-built building, the most modern in the complex. It serves as the national TB reference laboratory for the country and also as an approved supernational TB reference laboratory for the WHO.

Surveillance of the distribution of TB in the country, with a special focus on the 'hot spots' – that is, areas of concentrated transmission – is carried out with up-to-date geospatial techniques (data that are directly linked to geolocation).[65] In this way, these foci of concentrated transmission of the organism can be identified to optimally utilise the required interventions.

The crisis of antimicrobial resistance is particularly alarming with TB. The bacterium has developed high levels of resistance to anti-tuberculosis drugs.[66] TB bacteria that developed resistance to two of the most important anti-TB drugs, isoniazid and rifampicin, are referred to by the term MDR TB (multidrug-resistant TB). A further stage of resistance, XDR TB (extensively drug-resistant TB), goes even further, with additional resistance to further fallback drugs. Fortunately, XDR TB is considerably rarer but of course far more concerning and particularly challenging to treat. Specialised molecular studies using advanced instrumentation, such as next-generation whole genome sequencing, are being used to investigate the mechanisms of this drug resistance, and also to help understand the transmission patterns of the organism.

Monitoring the HIV/AIDS pandemic

In 2021 it was estimated that some 7.5 million people were living with HIV in South Africa, approximately 13 per cent of the total population of the country and the largest burden of HIV in the world.[67] The majority, nearly 4.8 million people, are on ART, making it the largest ART programme in the world and the most extensive monitoring programme in the world.

UNAIDS, the Joint United Nations Programme on HIV/AIDS, has proposed three targets for the eventual control of the HIV pandemic globally. These are referred to as the 90-90-90 targets – 90 per cent of individuals knowing their HIV status; 90 per cent of individuals living with HIV receiving ART; and 90 per cent being virally suppressed.[68]

A number of programmes have been created at the NICD to monitor the success of the management of HIV in the country and its progress towards reaching those 90-90-90 targets.[69] The earliest HIV surveillance programme, currently in its 30th year, is the antenatal seroprevalence programme. Samples of blood from over 1 500 sentinel sites, such as antenatal clinics, throughout the country, are sent to the NICD for HIV testing.[70] The prevalence has stabilised among young women at about 30 per cent, and an analysis of the 2017 report shows some signs of declining infection rates among very vulnerable 15- to 24-year-old women. Currently, the first and third targets have been met: 94.5 per cent of individuals living with HIV are aware of their status; 77.4 per cent of them are on ART – and in 91.5 per cent of those on treatment there is suppression of the virus.[71] The first of the 90-90-90 targets was reached by 2019,[72] but the third target has not yet been reached, mainly because of the worrying degree of resistance to antiretroviral (ARV) drugs.

The HIV drug-resistance laboratory of the NICD is the designated national surveillance laboratory and it also serves as a WHO regional HIV drug resistance laboratory and a quality control reference centre.[73] Advanced molecular sequencing technologies are being used to diagnose resistance to specific ARV drugs; in addition, next-generation sequencing is being employed to characterise and understand the mutations responsible for specific drug resistance. A more recent study of specimens of remnant blood sent for diagnostic viral load testing (testing to quantitate the amount of virus still remaining after treatment) showed that in 13 per cent of the specimens the virus was inadequately suppressed. Worryingly, in some 72 per cent of the latter, the virus could be shown to be resistant to ART.[74] (Remnant blood specimens are samples that are left over from specimens sent to clinical laboratories after they have been used for diagnostic testing.)

Surveillance for zoonotic pathogens

The term 'zoonosis' is used to indicate those organisms that are endemic in a non-human animal species, and which may, on occasion, cross the species barrier to infect humans. These cross-species infections are sporadic events usually involving individuals at risk of exposure to animals. Sometimes, following a sporadic infection of a human, a zoonotic agent, be it a virus, a bacterium or a parasite, may be transmitted between humans and subsequently may become established in the human population. Many pathogenic organisms have used this route to become human pathogens. With humans encroaching to an increasing extent into remote animal ecosystems through exploration, deforestation or the illegal trade of exotic animals, the risk of new emerging human pathogens from zoonotic origins has increased markedly in recent times. Examples range from HIV[75] to Covid-19.[76] It has been estimated that about 65 per cent of emerging communicable diseases over the past 60 years have been attributed to zoonotic agents. In recent times a One Health initiative has been created to better monitor for early signs of impending zoonotic-driven pandemics.[77] One Health aims to promote interconnectedness and collaboration between human and animal health experts and environmental scientists.

The most ancient and the most feared of the zoonotic diseases is rabies, known to humankind since 2000 BCE. It is the most lethal of all communicable diseases, with a mortality rate of almost 100 per cent once clinical symptoms become apparent. (And yet there is an effective vaccine for both humans and animals: the rabies vaccine, developed in 1885 by Louis Pasteur. It was the second vaccine ever to be used in humans.)

The NICD, in addition to providing a diagnostic service for this dreaded disease, also charts the distribution of the disease in the country. In South Africa, between 5 and 20 cases of rabies are diagnosed annually in five provinces – KwaZulu-Natal, Eastern Cape, Mpumalanga, Free State and Limpopo. The great majority of cases result from dog bites or exposure to saliva from infected dogs.

Surveillance of rodents from throughout the country plays an important role in the investigation of a variety of pathogens, including the ancient disease of plague, which is still present in South Africa, especially in the Eastern Cape.

Another animal routinely monitored at the NICD is the bat. Bats have been shown to be a major reservoir of serious human communicable diseases, from Ebola to Covid-19.[78] Regular expeditions by teams from the NICD trap bats from selected localities in the country. The NICD also houses a bat colony for research on these crucially important potential reservoirs of formidable communicable agents.

Surveillance of mosquitoes for carriage of arboviruses (viruses which are carried by arthropods) was one of the earliest surveillance activities in the NIV and then subsequently the NICD. Specially designed mosquito traps are placed in selected locations in the country. These mosquitoes are brought to the NICD laboratories to investigate whether they are carrying any arboviruses of human importance. Mosquitoes that are purposely bred for these investigations are infected with various arboviruses to examine the ability of specific species of mosquito to be vectors (carriers) and a potential source of infection to humans.

Malaria

The most important of the mosquito-borne communicable diseases on the African continent is malaria. Worldwide, the WHO estimated in

2020 that there were 241 million cases with between 440 000 and 627 000 people dying of the disease, predominantly children. Africa is home to 90 per cent of the world's burden of disease.[79]

Fortunately, in South Africa control measures against the anopheline mosquito have been successful and the disease is now considerably less common than elsewhere on the continent. Between 10 000 and 30 000 cases of malaria are notified annually in the country. The endemic regions coincide with the border areas in the three provinces of KwaZulu-Natal, Mpumalanga and Limpopo.[80] Seasonally, the risk increases between September and May. Malaria also occurs occasionally in non-endemic areas when infected mosquitoes are transported from endemic areas by road in minibus taxis and other vehicles. The delay in diagnosis contributes to greater mortality, over 10 times in some years, than regular malaria. Non-endemic malaria, also known as Odyssean malaria, emphasises the clinical importance of early diagnosis in the treatment of the disease.[81]

South Africa's Department of Health targeted 2023 for the elimination of local transmission of malaria. There were several challenges to meeting this target, however, including the continuing importation of cases from neighbouring endemic countries as well as difficulties in delivering insecticide-spraying programmes to the endemic areas in South Africa.[82] In addition, the bogey of the development of drug resistance, the bane of antimicrobial and antiviral therapy, reared its head with increasing insecticide resistance, which seriously hampers the control of malaria-carrying anopheline mosquitoes.

The anopheline mosquito is the subject of extensive in-depth research at the NICD. Studies on captive and colony-bred mosquitoes are carried out in three large purpose-built buildings, called insectaries, on the campus. Both temperature and humidity are carefully controlled inside these buildings, where colonies for breeding and experimental infection are maintained. Malaria surveillance involves assessing the ability of different species of mosquito, identified under the microscope, to act as carriers of malaria. Monitoring these mosquitoes for insecticide resistance and studying the mechanisms of this resistance are also essential components of the research activities in the insectaries.

Given the growth of insecticide resistance as well as the challenges in adequate reach of the spraying programmes,[83] alternate control strategies are also being researched. One of these is the sterile insect technique.[84] Studies of the biology of male mosquitoes have provided clues to strategies for the control of mosquito breeding by sterilisation of male mosquitoes.[85] Field trials releasing sterilised males into the environment are currently under investigation.

BUILDING CAPACITY FOR COMMUNICABLE DISEASES EPIDEMIOLOGY

The Field Epidemiology Training Programme (FETP) is the most important tool in creating a worldwide skilled and well-trained network of field epidemiologists.[86] The programme was an initiative of the CDC in the US and began in 1980. Between 1980 and 2020, over 18 000 disease detectives in more than 80 countries were trained through the programme. The FETP is a component of a global network of such training courses called TEPHINET (Training Programs in Epidemiology and Public Health Interventions Network), with AFENET (African Field Epidemiology Network) being the African component.

In 2006 the NICD, together with the CDC, established an FETP training programme. Subsequently, a laboratory component was added to the course, and the programme then became known as the SAFELTP (South African Field Epidemiology and Laboratory Training Programme). Close to 100 graduates have been through the programme, many from elsewhere on the African continent. The culmination of the training programme is the awarding of a master's degree in public health (MPH) from the University of Pretoria or a master's degree in epidemiology (MSc) from the University of the Witwatersrand. Trainees come into the programme with a health-oriented qualification; the majority are medical doctors, scientists or veterinarians.

As the name implies, the scope of the training programme is field epidemiology: that is, applying epidemiological science and technology to on-the-ground communicable disease as well as non-communicable disease health threats The course is predominantly a hands-on experiential training programme with students taking active roles in the management of outbreaks as well as participating in surveillance programmes.

The majority, some 75 per cent, of the graduates remain in the public service, contributing to the surveillance of and response to communicable diseases in the country.

5

The viral haemorrhagic fevers of Africa

T *he Andromeda Strain* (1969), *Outbreak* (1995), *Pandemic* (2020) and several other books and movies have captured the public's fascination with and fear of deadly infectious agents. The combination of high fever with copious production of blood and a rapidly fatal infectious disease are the essential ingredients of horror science fiction. However, they came to real-life reality with the advent of the feared and formidable viral haemorrhagic fevers.

The African viral haemorrhagic fevers, the most formidable of all, with mortalities approaching 90 per cent, sowed considerable alarm and fear in South Africa when some cases were sporadically imported into Johannesburg. It was the initial imported case in 1975 that triggered the establishment of the NIV. The highly specialised maximum-security laboratory, the only one on the continent, soon became a world leader in handling and investigating these viruses. The staff of the Special Pathogens Unit (SPU) have ventured into some of the most inhospitable places on earth to help control outbreaks of the disease and have significantly advanced research into these frightening infectious agents.

THE AFRICAN HAEMORRHAGIC FEVER THREAT

The first alarm bell

The drama of the first viral haemorrhagic fever on South African soil began rather quaintly – at a dinner party in February 1975. Professor James Gear was hosting the associate director of the Rockefeller Foundation for dinner at his home. The party was about to sit down to dinner when Gear's son, Dr John Gear, a consultant physician at the Johannesburg Hospital, arrived at the house, still in hospital scrubs and greatly worried about a patient in his care. The patient was a 20-year-old Australian man who presented with a high fever, a very sore throat, vomiting blood and bleeding from needle puncture wounds. That put an end to the dinner party with Gear and his guest hurrying to the hospital to examine the patient.

The man and his female companion had hitchhiked through Zimbabwe, sleeping on occasion out in the open and coming into contact with monkeys and a civet cat. Despite intensive treatment, the young man died a few days after admission. His companion soon became gravely ill with a similar presentation but survived, as did the attending nursing sister looking after them who subsequently also became infected.

Initially, thoughts turned to malaria or possibly yellow fever, but tests for these two communicable agents were negative. The possibility of a case of imported Lassa fever was then entertained, given the high fever, the sore throat and extensive bleeding from mucous membranes. Lassa fever is a viral haemorrhagic fever spread by the *Mastomys* rat indigenous to West Africa. However, it was the electron microscopic examination of post-mortem tissue at the PRF laboratories that revealed the causal agent to be the Marburg virus.[87]

Where exactly this young man became infected still remains a mystery, despite an intensive search carried out all along the hitchhiking route. The reservoir host of Marburg is the Egyptian fruit bat, *Rousettus aegyptiacus*, which is found widely throughout Africa. Was it contact with the monkeys, or the civet cat while he was asleep?

The need for specialist measures

It was this first episode of an African viral haemorrhagic fever in South Africa that alerted health officials in the government to the need for a special biohazard isolation facility to be created to nurse patients suspected to be infected with these formidable communicable agents. This was particularly important given the high volume of migrants coming from countries to the north of South Africa, especially those employed in the mining industry. In addition, because of the high lethality of these biological agents, a specialised, highly sophisticated BSL-4 laboratory would need to be constructed for diagnostic and research purposes.[88]

The incident marked the launch of one of the major divisions of the NIV, and later, the NICD's SPU. The activities of the unit were focused on the viral haemorrhagic diseases, rabies, and also those viruses transmitted to humans by arthropods (arboviruses). In common parlance one would refer to arthropods as 'bugs'. In technical parlance arthropods are a large phylum of animals characterised by having an outer skeleton and jointed limbs. Examples of medical importance are insects such as ticks, bedbugs and spiders.

Historically, the activities and the experience of the SPU date back to the early years of the Second World War. A medical officer of the South African Defence Force, a young Major James Gear, later to become the first director of the PRF laboratories, was sent to the Rockefeller Institute for Medical Research in New York to work on the arbovirus yellow fever, under Max Theiler (the first South African Nobel laureate). Gear spent eight months in New York, returning to South Africa in October 1942 to establish the yellow fever vaccine production facility. The US-produced yellow fever vaccine, together with locally produced typhus vaccine, was supplied to Allied troops fighting in various theatres of the war.

Thus was the groundwork laid for the arbovirus unit, which was then within the SAIMR. Over the subsequent years, the unit gained widespread experience and international recognition for its work. When the NIV came into being in 1976, the unit was already a major division of the institute as the SPU. In 1980 Professor Robert (Bob) Swanepoel, who had established the medical and veterinary laboratories in Zimbabwe, was recruited to head the SPU with its newly established maximum-security BSL-4 laboratory.

The BSL-4 laboratory

The first BSL-4 laboratory in the world was constructed at the CDC in Atlanta in 1967, in response to the Marburg outbreaks in Germany and Yugoslavia. In a repeat of history, it was the Marburg incident of 1975 in Johannesburg that triggered the development of the BSL-4 laboratory at the NIV/NICD, the first and only BSL-4 laboratory on the African continent.

Despite the international political ostracism of the country at the time, contact was made with personnel at the CDC, and one of their engineers who had been involved in the construction of that laboratory was contracted to assist in the design of the South African facility. Construction was completed in 1979 and the facility was commissioned in 1980.

Essentially, a BSL-4 laboratory is a highly sophisticated engineering structure specifically designed and constructed to enable laboratory and experimental work to be carried out on the most dangerous of communicable agents, with punctilious attention to all precautionary details to ensure the safety of the personnel working in this environment.

The laboratory consists of two sections – a cabinet line and a suit laboratory. The cabinet line is a collection of steel biological cabinets connected in series to each other. The cabinets are hermetically sealed and work within each of the cabinets is carried out through sealed glove boxes. Specimens and biological materials are introduced through an opening hatch and are then passed from cabinet to cabinet to reach the relevant working cabinet. The space inside the cabinets is kept under negative pressure as an additional safety measure in the unlikely event of a leak. Furthermore, the flow of the evacuating air passes through a HEPA (high-efficiency particulate air) filter to remove, through filtration, any viral particles. In addition, ultraviolet lamps are switched on when the cabinet is not in use to inactivate any possible remnant communicable disease agents. As can be imagined, passing material along the line of cabinets through the glove boxes of each cabinet is rather cumbersome and somewhat inefficient. In practice, the cabinet line is seldom used and the major portion of the BSL-4 work is carried out in the second component, the suit laboratory.

The suit laboratory conjures up images of space travel. To protect personnel in this laboratory, they need first to climb into a hermetically sealed, full-body plastic suit. Air for breathing and cooling is supplied by connecting the back of the suit to a supply hose suspended from the ceiling. To move through the laboratory, the operator disconnects and then connects up to the nearest suspended hose. An annexe of the suit laboratory is used for working with laboratory animals. On exiting the laboratory, the operator walks through a decontaminating shower which sprays disinfectant onto the surface of the suit.

When commissioned, the BSL-4 laboratory was only one of a handful of such facilities in the world and it is still the only stand-alone BSL-4 laboratory on the African continent. Originally intended to be a reference and diagnostic centre for the Southern African region, it was not long before its value and use as an early warning diagnostic centre was established for the entire African continent and further afield. In 2002 it was made a WHO regional collaborating centre for viral haemorrhagic fevers and arboviruses.

SURVEILLANCE OF AFRICAN VIRAL HAEMORRHAGIC FEVERS

The BSL-4 laboratory soon became the critical clearing house to screen for the dangerous agents of haemorrhagic fevers. Specimens from patients with an acute onset of fever and a bleeding tendency are regularly sent to the laboratory to exclude these hazardous agents. Fortunately, the great majority turn out to have less alarming diagnoses, mostly bacterial septicaemia (often due to meningococcal infection), viral hepatitis, tickborne typhus, malaria and even AIDS.

Crimean-Congo haemorrhagic fever (CCHF)

The most common of the viral haemorrhagic fevers in Southern Africa was found to be Crimean-Congo haemorrhagic fever (CCHF).[89] The name derives from the geographic location in Crimea where Soviet scientists in 1944 first recognised it to be a viral disease in advancing Soviet troops towards the end of the Second World War. Subsequently, the causative virus was isolated in the then Belgian Congo in 1956. The infection was found to be endemic throughout Africa, the Middle East, Asia and the Balkans. Humans are infected either by being bitten by the common hard-bodied tick of the genus *Hyalomma*, or by direct contact with livestock. Transmission between humans is less common but may occur, particularly in a hospital situation.

The first recognised South African case of CCHF was diagnosed in February 1981 in a 13-year-old schoolboy.[90] A few days before this lad's illness he had been in a veld school sleeping out in the open. A *Hyalomma* tick, characteristically recognised by the typical banding pattern of its legs, was extracted from the boy's scalp. The offending tick may well have been previously feeding on antelope grazing in the luxuriant grass following good rains. Sadly, the youngster died three days after the onset of his illness. Specimens to confirm the diagnosis were among the first processed in the new BSL-4 laboratory.

In the ensuing 20 years, a total of 165 cases of CCHF were diagnosed in Southern Africa. In the main (71 of 165 cases, 43 per cent) the infections came from tick bites or from squashing ticks. Second in order (67 of 165 cases, 40.6 per cent) came from contact with blood or other infected biological material from livestock – for example, in abattoirs. A smaller number of cases (7 of 165 cases, 4.2 per cent) followed contact with infected patients. In the remainder of the cases (20 of 165 cases, 12.1 per cent) the origin was not clear, although most of these patients lived in rural areas. The mortality rate from CCHF fluctuated between 25 and 30 per cent.

Marburg and Ebola haemorrhagic fevers

The BSL-4 laboratory received more publicity for its involvement with the higher-profile viral haemorrhagic fevers Marburg and Ebola. The SPU played a crucial role in providing diagnostic services for the continent and beyond. Members of the unit regularly visited the sites of these outbreaks and took part, with international teams, in the control of these outbreaks. Importantly, they also invested a great deal of energy in building local capacity.

In May and June of 1995, two members of the unit joined an international team from the CDC and the US Army Medical Research Institute of Infectious Diseases (USAMRID) to investigate and assist in the control of an outbreak of Ebola in Kikwit, Zaire, now the Democratic Republic of the Congo (DRC).[91] In the following year, 1996, Ebola (named after the Ebola River in the DRC) broke out both in the DRC and in southern Sudan. The virus is among the most deadly of infectious organisms. It carried a mortality rate in that outbreak of 88 per cent in the DRC and 53 per cent in Sudan. The SPU, together with international facilities, was able to provide early diagnoses and rapid responses to the African viral haemorrhagic fevers. Outbreaks of both Marburg and Ebola started being recognised with increased frequency in many countries in Africa.

Ebola in South Africa

The first Ebola case in South Africa was diagnosed in November 1996, in upmarket Sandton, immediately north of Johannesburg. It involved a 46-year-old nursing sister who had looked after a patient, a medical doctor, who had arrived in South Africa from Gabon, West Africa, for treatment. Initially, the patient was thought to be suffering from hepatitis, despite the presence of a high fever. The attending nursing sister took ill and, despite intensive efforts to save her, she passed away four days later. Unbeknown to the South African medical personnel at the time of the doctor-patient's admission to the South African hospital, he had been treating Ebola patients in Gabon shortly before arriving in South Africa. Specimens sent to the BSL-4 laboratory confirmed the diagnosis of Ebola. He made a full recovery.

As a result of this episode, the hospital was closed, and some 350 potential contacts were placed under quarantine. Fortunately, there was no further spread. Not surprisingly, the episode, fuelled by the dramatic coverage in the media, generated considerable alarm and consternation in the general public, and there was serious concern that the episode could materially threaten South Africa's important tourism industry.

Massive Marburg and Ebola outbreaks in Africa

In 1998 the DRC was to experience a massive outbreak of Marburg in a village called Durba in the north-east of the country.[92] The region at the time was under rebel occupation and the site of the outbreak was an illegal gold mine where miners were exposed to bats and rats in the underground workings. The outbreak was extensive, with a high mortality rate of 81.6 per cent (115 deaths out of 141 cases), including some secondary cases passed on to household contacts. In 2005, the largest and the deadliest outbreak of Marburg ever recorded took place in Angola, with its epicentre in the Uige Province in the north-west of the country.[93] Of the 374 cases diagnosed, 329 died – a frighteningly high case fatality rate of 88 per cent. Personnel from the SPU assisted a multinational team from several countries in the diagnosis and control of that outbreak.

Ebola has also far from disappeared in Africa, in particular in Central and West Africa. Scattered outbreaks, independent of each other, continued throughout the region in 2001 and 2002. The source of these infections was thought to come from the locals consuming bushmeat – chiefly chimpanzees, gorillas and duiker. Unfortunately, investigations were hampered by the hostility of the locals to outsider medical teams.

Two years later, in Sierra Leone, West Africa, the SPU again played a critical role in the surveillance, investigation and control of another outbreak of African haemorrhagic fever. This time it was the 2014/2015 massive outbreak of Ebola – arguably the most severe ever recorded.[94] In August 2014 the WHO declared the epidemic an international public health emergency. The staff of the NICD's SPU established an Ebola mobile laboratory in Sierra Leone and played a crucial role in the diagnosis and control of the outbreak, processing over 7 000 suspected cases.[95] In addition, they carried out extensive training of local personnel and then handed over the emergency mobile laboratory to the country so that operations could continue until the outbreak was over. The mobile lab would also serve as a rapid diagnostic laboratory for any future outbreaks.

The infection spread to neighbouring Guinea and Liberia, and sporadic cases were imported into the US, UK and Spain from healthcare worker contacts. The epidemic was finally brought under control and declared no longer to be an emergency in March 2016. The disease re-appeared, however, both in West and Central Africa and localised outbreaks continue to this day.

The impact of the outbreaks in Sierra Leone, Guinea and Liberia, over and above the tragic burden of the illness and the loss of life, was massive in economic terms. Over US$2.2 billion, according to the World Bank, was used to control the outbreak and a further US$162 billion was funnelled into the countries for recovery.

The unique Lujo outbreak in Southern Africa

A noteworthy virological discovery by the SPU took place in September and October of 2008.[96] A female travel guide took seriously ill with symptoms of a viral haemorrhagic fever in September in Lusaka, Zambia, and was airlifted to Johannesburg for treatment. Despite intensive treatment, she died two days later. A hospital cleaner who cleaned the ward also succumbed. Three other contacts – two nurses and a paramedic – also contracted the infection and became ill, but survived. The causative virus, isolated in the BSL-4 laboratory, had never been seen previously and the SPU gave it the name Lujo virus – combining the first two letters of Lusaka and Johannesburg. Mysteriously, the virus has never been seen since.

The SPU response to outbreaks nationally and internationally

In conclusion, the story of the SPU extends far beyond the African haemorrhagic fevers. The arbovirus unit and the rabies unit together with the BSL-4 laboratory have provided diagnostic and research services not only to South Africa but also to over 23 countries on the African continent and over 10 countries in Europe, Asia, the Middle East and as far afield as Afghanistan. The value of this remarkable unit has been widely appreciated, not only by the WHO's recognition of it as a regional collaborating centre but also by major international organisations responsible for global health. Some of the pivotal advances in our understanding of the ecology and epidemiology of these elusive and often deadly viruses have come from these studies, often carried out in many field expeditions with staff frequently venturing into some of the most inhospitable regions of the continent.

An Emergency Operations Centre (EOC) was created in the NICD in 2015 to support the pivotal role of the SPU in responding to biological threats to the country and the region, The facility is modelled on similar facilities operating in the CDC as well as in several countries in Europe and North America. It is equipped with state-of-the-art technology to gather epidemiological information and co-ordinate emergency responses to communicable disease threats, including the African haemorrhagic fevers.

6

Facing the HIV/AIDS pandemic

At the close of the twentieth century, medical science could look back with a great deal of satisfaction on many outstanding achievements and successes in the control of communicable diseases. Confidence in controlling the bulk of communicable disease threats rose with the availability and effectiveness of an increasing number of preventive vaccines and therapeutic advances.

However, as the century was coming to a close there arose one of the most menacing of communicable diseases. This relentless plague, which would progressively and inexorably expand its reach into the human population, was HIV/AIDS. By the end of the century, South Africa came to carry the heaviest burden of the pandemic, with the largest number of people living with the infection in the world and driving the largest HIV/AIDS treatment programme globally.[97] Close to one in five adults (15 to 49 years of age) are infected with the virus. The figure is even more frightening in some sections of the population, especially young women in KwaZulu-Natal, where the prevalence of infection is as high as one in three.

Some 40 years after the discovery of the virus the cumulative global death toll from HIV/AIDS, as of the end of 2021, stood at 40.1 million.[98]

Given South Africa's disease burden, it is not surprising, therefore, that the HIV/AIDS research unit is the largest research unit in the NICD. It has contributed enormously to the understanding of the virus and the disease, as well as making important contributions to research efforts into developing the elusive protective vaccine. Unfortunately, political interference, yet again, had a turn in meddling in the activities of this unit, and in so doing wasted valuable resources, energy and time while the epidemic was advancing rapidly in the population. Support for dissident anti-science was fortunately temporary, but at the time it became a worrying reputational embarrassment.

THE EARLY DAYS OF THE PANDEMIC

The saga of HIV/AIDS commenced rather unobtrusively in Los Angeles in the autumn of 1980. An alert physician, Michael Gottlieb, and his colleagues were intrigued by the unusual presentation of a cluster of five young male patients under their care who were all diagnosed with a very uncommon form of pneumonia due to a parasite called *Pneumocystis carinii*.[99] Previously, this infection had been seen almost exclusively in patients whose immune systems had been severely depressed, either by disease or drugs used in transplant recipients or patients on cancer therapy.

The following year, the CDC reported in their weekly bulletin, the *Morbidity and Mortality Weekly Report* (*MMWR*), of 5 June 1981, an account of a collection of 26 men in New York and California diagnosed with a rare tumour called Kaposi's sarcoma, which was found almost exclusively in gay young men.[100]

The NIV, in common with many academic institutions, had a journal club where medical and scientific staff would present and discuss the contents of up-to-date publications in scientific journals. In one of these meetings in mid 1981, the presentation of the day was the *MMWR* publication of 5 June. At the time it was no more than an interesting curiosity – what is sometimes referred to in medical parlance as a 'canary'.

The picture was soon to change dramatically. A clinical definition of the malady was established and in 1983 the incriminating virus, HIV, was isolated at the Pasteur Institute, France, by Nobel laureates Luc Montagnier and Françoise Barré-Sinoussi.[101] A year later, a team from the US under the leadership of Robert Gallo isolated and propagated HIV (which they initially called HTLV-3[102]).[103] A spirited interchange ensued with political overtones between the French and the American teams as to who were the original discoverers of the virus – and thus entitled to intellectual ownership. It was ultimately settled with the sharing of intellectual property rights.

A laboratory diagnostic test could now be designed and was soon widely available to chart the spread of the infection. And spread it did! Inexorably, the epidemic advanced into North America and Europe, taking a progressively increasing toll, chiefly among gay men and intravenous drug users.

Early in 1986 alert physicians in Belgium and France similarly became aware of the syndrome in African patients.[104] However, unlike the patients in North America and Europe, where the disease was found mainly in gay men, often combined with the use of recreational drugs, in Africa it occurred predominantly in heterosexual males and females.

Indications from what are termed sero-archaeological studies[105] suggest that the virus originated in the past in Africa. Tests on specimens stored in refrigerators revealed the earliest positive result in a blood specimen from a man who died in 1959 in Kinshasa in the then Belgian Congo.[106] Further studies of the history of HIV were carried out on close to a million genomes stored in the HIV database at the Los Alamos National Laboratory in the US.[107] The changes in the sequence of the building blocks of the genome can be related to the evolution of the virus over time – what is referred to as the 'molecular clock'. These analyses indicate that HIV was originally from Africa and was a zoonosis[108] (as was the case with SARS-CoV-2 and the viral haemorrhagic diseases discussed in the previous chapter); it was estimated to have crossed the species barrier from primates, such as chimpanzees, to humans in the early 1930s.[109]

HIV/AIDS IN SOUTH AFRICA

South Africa saw its first patients with HIV/AIDS in 1982.[110] Two patients, gay men, both flight attendants, were diagnosed at autopsy at the University of Pretoria to have died of AIDS.

For several years thereafter no cases were identified in the country. Interestingly, a study in 1986 at the NICD failed to detect evidence of HIV infection in a sample of drug abusers.[111] Even more remarkable, a study which we published from the NICD in 1987 was tellingly entitled 'Absence of HIV Infection in Prostitutes and Women Attending Sexually-Transmitted Diseases Clinics in South Africa'.[112]

Fortunately, the health authorities in South Africa were responsive to calls from the NIV and did anticipate the gathering clouds of the forth-coming catastrophic HIV/AIDS epidemic, soon to severely strike the country. In early 1987, even with not a great deal of evidence of disease at that time, the NIV succeeded in being awarded a Medical Research Council AIDS virus research unit. This fledgling unit soon became the largest research unit in the NIV, and later the NICD.

In 1990 the NIV, together with the Department of Health, began an annual study of the prevalence of HIV in samples from women attending antenatal clinics throughout the country to chart the entrance and spread of the virus. The percentage of women who were HIV positive in 1990, as determined from these samples, was 0.7 per cent. In 1991, the tally of reported AIDS cases passed the 1 000 mark, although preliminary extrapolations from the seroprevalence data estimated the reservoir of HIV-infected individuals to exceed 300 000.[113]

Already at this time, it was clear that heterosexually spread HIV infection would, by far, dominate the South African HIV/AIDS landscape. By 1991, 46 per cent of cases were heterosexually spread as against 36 per cent homosexually and 15 per cent paediatric (mainly children infected from their mothers at birth).

HIV infection expanded steeply and within a decade sub-Saharan Africa, and South Africa, became the global epicentre of the HIV/AIDS pandemic, with the highest number of people infected with the virus of any country in the world. By 1998, the antenatal survey revealed that one in five women country-wide – and in KwaZulu-Natal Province one in three women – were found to be infected with HIV.[114]

The tragedy of HIV/AIDS denial

The late 1980s witnessed the beginnings of what was to become one of the most bizarre and lamentable chapters in the public health history of South Africa. What was especially tragic was that this was precisely the time when ARV drugs were starting to show clear benefits in treating AIDS. The NIV was unwillingly and inescapably dragged into a woefully wasteful quagmire of HIV/AIDS dissidence and the saga of the South African government's denialism.

The champion of AIDS denialism was none other than the second president of democratic South Africa, Thabo Mbeki. What precisely drove the president to take a position totally against overwhelming scientific evidence and truth is still difficult to understand. Was he motivated by the grotesque spectre of South Africa leading the world in its toll of HIV/AIDS and manifesting itself, particularly, in the black African population? (A 2008 study by the Human Sciences Research Council found an infection rate of 13 per cent among black Africans as compared to 0.3 per cent in whites.[115])

Perhaps it was an attempt to address the HIV/AIDS problem in Africa by an 'African' rather than a 'Western' initiative – a view Mbeki propounded and repeatedly articulated in a five-page letter to US President Bill Clinton and United Nations Secretary General Kofi Annan, as well as in his opening speech in 2000 at the International AIDS Conference in Durban.[116] Perhaps it was the vocal South African denialist Anthony Brink, a non-medical lawyer, who described one of the earlier anti-HIV agents, AZT, as toxic and ineffective. Or perhaps he was influenced by the high-profile American Christine Maggiore, whom he had met in the mid 90s.

The story of Christine Maggiore is one of the most tragic and poignant to come out of the early history of HIV/AIDS. She also happened to be one of the guests of Mbeki at the 2000 International AIDS Conference and may well have played an early role in moulding his unorthodox views on AIDS. Maggiore was an American freelance consultant to the US government. She tested positive for HIV in 1992 as part of a routine medical examination. Influenced by the prominent AIDS denialist Peter Duesberg, she questioned the implications of her positive HIV test and, as a result, refused treatment, opting instead for a naturopathic programme. Rebuffing medical advice, she defiantly breastfed her children, claiming she was in excellent health. Her youngest child took ill in 2005 and died a month later of opportunistic infections characteristic of AIDS. In mid 2008 Maggiore developed pneumonia and in December of that year died of disseminated herpes and candida infection characteristic of terminal AIDS. She was 52 years old.

While still deputy president, Mbeki lobbied for the deployment of a South African anti-AIDS 'drug', which was indeed toxic, called Virodene.[117] This industrial solvent, known chemically as dimethyl-formamide, was promoted by President Mbeki as being far cheaper than medically approved drugs. It was also one developed in South Africa and not a product of the Western medical establishment. Unsurprisingly, and despite claims being touted from a few illegal 'trials', registration of the miracle solvent was rejected by the then South African Medicines Control Council (MCC) (now the South African Health Products Regulatory Authority, or SAHPRA). Professor Peter Folb, emeritus professor of pharmacology at the University of Cape Town, served as chairman of the MCC for 18 years. He strenuously opposed strong government pressure to register Virodene. His principled and scientific stand resulted in him being dismissed as chairman of the MCC. The registrar and deputy registrar of the MCC suffered the same fate.

On 14 June 1999, Thabo Mbeki was inaugurated as South Africa's second democratically elected president. It soon became abundantly clear that he was going to drive a troubling HIV/AIDS denial agenda. Supported by well-known HIV/AIDS denialists, Mbeki propounded the narrative that AIDS was not due to a virus but was the direct result of poverty and malnutrition. Alarmed by the devastating effect that AIDS denialism could have on the future management of the most serious disease of the subcontinent, the scientific community, both in South Africa and abroad, rallied with a flurry of letters, opinion pieces and editorials in the scientific literature.[118]

On 6 July 2000, *Nature* published the Durban Declaration, which was a response to the AIDS denialism that had taken root in the South African government.[119] The declaration was designed to coincide with the 13th International AIDS Conference in Durban, the premier conference on AIDS, attended by over 5 000 of the leading workers in the field. The document was drawn up and signed by over 5 000 eminent scientists, including 11 Nobel laureates. To be a signatory to the declaration one had to have graduated with, at the least, a doctorate, and also have no commercial interests.

There was much anticipation that, given the volume and the level of anxiety felt by the scientific community internationally, the president would respect and accept established scientific wisdom and knowledge when he opened the conference in Durban on 9 July. But, as his speech unfolded, hopes came crashing down.[120] Reminiscent of the letter he sent to Bill Clinton and Kofi Annan, the report lacked any mention of the HI virus, but a great deal was made of poverty and malnutrition being the cause of AIDS. A prominent article in the previous Sunday's *Sunday Independent* newspaper, written by the newly appointed minister of health, Dr Manto Tshabalala-Msimang, and two other cabinet ministers, entitled 'Mbeki's Stand on AIDS was Dictated by African Realities', defended the president's standpoint.[121]

Compounding the anxieties of the scientific world internationally and within the country, the minister of health embarked on a vigorous programme eschewing medically endorsed regimens for treating HIV/AIDS. Rather, it was to be traditional African natural remedies of vegetables and herbs that were promoted – earning for herself the nickname 'Dr Beetroot' – while access to medically approved drugs was denied.

The president's AIDS Advisory Panel

To try to make the abandonment of scientific medicine in favour of indigenous natural remedies look more respectable, the president announced at the Durban conference that he would be establishing a Presidential AIDS Advisory Panel of international and local experts. The task of the panel was ostensibly to be an objective inquiry and investigation, tasked with objectively and 'scientifically' examining both the denialist as well as the conventional scientific narrative concerning HIV/AIDS. The terms of reference were essentially twofold: was AIDS caused by the HI virus, and should it be treated with ARV drugs?

The panel met on two occasions, in Pretoria on 6 and 7 May 2000, and two months later, in Johannesburg on 3 and 4 July. The local and international delegates were represented more or less equally by AIDS denialists and scientists who accepted international wisdom. The first session was attended by 32 delegates and the second session by 45 delegates.

The denialists were undoubtedly a colourful and disparate group, ranging in background from the renowned cancer molecular biologist Professor Peter Duesberg[122] to a historian, Professor Charles Geshekter.[123] Among themselves, they took up different positions. Duesberg was able to accept that HIV did exist, but insisted that it was a common harmless virus and not the cause of AIDS. Others were more radical. An electron microscopist from Australia, Eleni Papadopoulos-Eliopoulos, doggedly maintained that there was no proof that the HI virus even existed.

The panel's deliberations were published in March 2001 in a 134-page report.[124] Unsurprisingly, it made very little contribution to the scientific literature. Essentially, the report was simply a record of the presentations that reviewed the scientific knowledge of HIV/AIDS of the time, together with the denialists rebutting the validity of the laboratory evidence of the science. The meetings themselves were nothing more than a rowdy, often unpleasant gathering characterised by interjections, heckling and derision. The more intrusive and louder voices came from the denialists, who frequently interrupted and overrode the more measured attempts for rational discussion by the orthodox scientists.

Other than the report, the only outcome of the AIDS advisory panel was the notorious testing project – an exercise of very little scientific or public health value, but an exercise that was an abject squandering of time, energy and financial cost, especially to the NIV.

The testing project came from the AIDS denialist contingent who wanted to demonstrate that HIV-positive laboratory results in blood could well be due not to HIV but rather to antibodies directed against other organisms common in this part of the world. In other words, the diagnosis of HIV was falsely positive due to cross-reacting antibodies from other infecting agents. By implication, there was no evidence that HIV was the cause of clinical AIDS.

The experimental proposal was to adsorb out these cross-reacting antibodies by pre-coating the testing plastic plates with material extracted from these cross-reacting organisms. A list of a dozen of these allegedly cross-reacting communicable agents was drawn up – amoebae, various bacteria and viruses. A panel of 2 447 HIV-positive serum samples was collected from laboratories throughout the country and subjected to these pre-absorption 'experiments'.

It was no surprise to the orthodox scientists that the experiments failed to produce any meaningful information other than that it was a colossal, fruitless expenditure. Equally not surprising was the reaction of the denialist team, spearheaded by Dr Harvey Bialy, an American molecular biologist, who also wrote a biography of Peter Duesberg. Criticising the experiment itself, he wrote to me: 'Barry, what does it mean the pre-absorption experiments will be carried out as YOU wrote them????? Sorry my friend, they will be carried out as WE wrote them. Got it??????'[125] Perhaps even closer to the tone of the collegial interchange, Harvey penned off a letter to my colleague Professor Carolyn Williamson, professor of virology at the University of Cape Town and also an unwillingly co-opted member of the notorious advisory panel, who had offered a comment on the meaninglessness of the exercise. 'Carolyn, your arrogance is matched only by your ignorance.'[126]

The Treatment Action Campaign (TAC)

Sadly, this exercise in futility foisted on the NIV by the government of the day wasted countless valuable person-hours during a particularly challenging time in the unfolding of the HIV epidemic in the country. But this abject wastage of energy and resources was overshadowed by a much bigger tragedy of that era of HIV/AIDS denialism.

The narrative ostensibly to find an African solution to this calamitous misfortune was, in reality, influenced and pursued with input from non-African, non-scientific mavericks from North America and other Western countries. The dissident yarn not only denied the viral cause of AIDS but, tragically, also attacked the use of antiviral drugs as being 'toxic'. A direct result of this lamentable course of action was published in a study carried out at the Harvard School of Public Health.[127] The authors calculated that over 330 000 lives were lost, and 3.8 million person-years of ARV treatment benefits were forfeited as a result of the denialist-fuelled refusal to promptly institute ARV treatment between 2000 and 2005.

Civil society fought a vigorous campaign against the calumny of HIV/AIDS denial. Most prominent was the Treatment Action Campaign (TAC), formed by Zackie Achmat and 10 other activists in December 1998, which played a crucial role in coercing a reluctant Mbeki government to commence providing ARV drugs and management programmes for people living with the virus. Support came from prominent national and international quarters, including former president Nelson Mandela and then senator Barack Obama. The courts of the country also played an important role, spearheaded by then Supreme Court justice Edwin Cameron.[128]

ARV drugs started to trickle into the country, but relief needed to await the resignation of Thabo Mbeki as president of South Africa and Minister of Health Dr Manto Tshabalala-Msimang, on 25 September 2008. Her successor, Barbara Hogan, instituted a radical change, pursuing a conventional and orthodox medical approach to HIV/AIDS. ARVs flowed into the country and the era of official HIV/AIDS denial mercifully came to an end. Not long after, South Africa instituted the largest and most comprehensive ARV programme in the world and took its place as a world leader in HIV/AIDS research.

Monitoring and researching HIV/AIDS

The Centre for HIV and STIs (CHIVSTI) is the largest of the six centres of the NICD, providing support for the enormous public health challenge of the HIV/AIDS epidemic in South Africa. The activities of this centre, as implied in the name, extend beyond HIV/AIDS to other viral and bacterial sexually transmitted infections.

Within this centre the largest section is the HIV/AIDS research unit. The unit was the first MRC-supported unit in the NICD, in 1988. Under the leadership of the distinguished researcher Professor Lynn Morris, the unit took its place as an international centre for HIV/AIDS research. Professor Morris later went on to become the director of the NICD from 2018 to 2020 and, subsequently, deputy vice-chancellor for research and innovation at the University of the Witwatersrand.

South Africa is well known for housing the world's largest number of people living with HIV – estimated in 2021 to be 8.2 million people, about 13.7 per cent of the total population.[129] (A more recent mathematical model estimated the number of people living with HIV in South Africa to be 7.8 million.[130]) In the adult 15- to 49-year-old age group, the figure rises to 19.5 per cent, or close to one in five young adults in South Africa who are living with HIV.

Addressing this formidable public health challenge is the largest ARV programme in the world, involving over 5.5 million people, about two-thirds of individuals calculated to be living with HIV. Supplying support to the assorted arms of this gargantuan venture are the various activities of the CHIVSTI. These range from epidemiological surveillance, providing reference diagnostic testing, and monitoring for resistance of the various drugs used in the treatment programmes for sexually transmitted infections.

Measuring the HIV/AIDS epidemic

The dynamics of the epidemic are charted through several programmes. The earliest and most extensive of these is the Antenatal HIV Sentinel Survey. Conducted annually since 1990, the survey aims to monitor the extent as well as the trends of HIV infection in women between the ages of 15 and 49 attending antenatal clinics throughout South Africa.

In scientific terms this is called a seroepidemiological study. It investigates the epidemiology of an infectious disease through the study of serum samples. It involves the planned collection of blood specimens from a population under investigation. Serum, the fluid left over after blood undergoes clotting, is tested for either the presence of a particular organism, in this case the HI virus, or the specific antibodies made by the defence mechanism of the body to combat the organism. Detection of these antibodies indicates present or past infection.

In 2019 some 37 116 pregnant women from 1 589 public health facilities in all 52 districts of South Africa had samples of blood tested for HIV and also for syphilis.[131] It was from this survey that the national antenatal HIV prevalence was estimated to be at 30 per cent and the prevalence of syphilis at 2.1 per cent.

How well is the country dealing with the formidable HIV/AIDS challenge? The upward trend in HIV infection in this population seems now to have stabilised over the past few years at the 30 per cent level. The effectiveness of some of the control programmes is measured against specific international standards. An example of one of these performance standards is the 90-90-90 initiative launched by UNAIDS.[132] As has already been discussed, the initiative established three goals: 90 per cent of all individuals living with HIV knowing their diagnosis; 90 per cent of those diagnosed with HIV being on treatment; and 90 per cent of those tested attaining suppression of the virus. In the most recent antenatal survey in the country, CHIVSTI demonstrated that the first two goals had been achieved.

In addition to these national surveys, the CHIVSTI examines the outcomes of specific implementation programmes aimed at reducing HIV incidence. For example, a targeted programme, appropriately identified by its acronym DREAMS (Determined, Resilient, Empowered, AIDS-free, Mentored and Safe), was introduced by the United States President's Emergency Plan for AIDS Relief (PEPFAR). The programme is directed at reducing the incidence of HIV among adolescent girls and young women.[133] Incidence rates in a number of these programme sites have varied from 0.75 per cent to 1.38 per cent.

Monitoring ARV drug resistance

HIV belongs to a group of viruses called retroviruses. These viruses are characterised by a unique replication process utilising an enzyme called reverse transcriptase. This enzyme reverses the normal sequence of replication of biological organisms: instead of the more conventional route of DNA to RNA to protein, the replication sequence of these viruses proceeds from RNA to DNA to RNA to protein (*retro* in Latin means 'backwards'). A number of the drugs used to treat HIV target the enzyme reverse transcriptase and are thus called antiretroviral drugs or ARVs.

The advent of ARV drugs to treat HIV has revolutionised the management of HIV infection. They have converted what was, in the early days of the epidemic, feared to be a universally fatal infection into a manageable chronic disease. Several ARV drugs have been used in treatment programmes and, over time, there have been significant improvements, both in the development of new and better drugs and also improvements in the regimens used for treatment.

As was discussed in Chapter 4, one of the gravest communicable disease threats is the development of resistance by micro-organisms and viruses to the drugs used in their treatment. HIV drug resistance is of particular concern. Being the most extensively mutating of all viruses, it is especially liable to develop resistance to ARV drugs. For this reason, virus isolates are regularly tested for the development of resistance to enable appropriate changes to be made to treatment.

The CHIVSTI is an accredited international reference laboratory of the WHO for ARV drug resistance. Testing for drug resistance is carried out on virus material recruited from the remnants of specimens sent to 16 of the routine clinical laboratories of the NHLS.[134] In 2019 it was found that some 72 per cent of patients with detectable virus in their blood, despite treatment, harboured resistant organisms.

HIV vaccine research

The ultimate Holy Grail of HIV/AIDS research is without doubt the development of a safe and effective preventive vaccine. The challenge was, and remains, enormous.[135] It was never envisaged to be so formidable and daunting a challenge when the virus was first isolated in 1983. As mentioned in the Introduction, a year after the successful isolation of the virus, the then US secretary of health, Dr Margaret Heckler, standing on a press conference platform with the co-discoverer of the HI virus, Dr Robert Gallo, predicted that a successful vaccine was only about two years away!

Thousands of the most talented scientists and researchers throughout the world, many of them in South Africa, including an outstanding team in the NICD, have yet to create a successful candidate vaccine after some 40 years of intensive research. Effectiveness trials of candidate vaccines, some in South Africa, have unfortunately fallen well short of producing even a potential prospect of developing into an effective vaccine.

Colleagues outside of the field of HIV/AIDS research are often perplexed as to why HIV vaccine research, despite a huge volume of scientific knowledge on the properties of the virus, has still failed to create even a potential opening to develop an effective vaccine, while vaccines against so many other communicable agents have been developed in modern times within a matter of a handful of years (or, in the case of the Covid-19 vaccine, even within a year).

Unfortunately, the two main barriers to a successful HIV vaccine have not yet been defeated. The first is the enormous changeability of the virus, which is vastly more changeable than any other virus. This singular property favours the selection of mutations, even in a single infected individual, enabling it effectively to escape the immune response. The second barrier is the virus's ability to infect cells in locations in the body that are inaccessible to the body's immune system, thereby effectively concealing the virus and protecting it from being neutralised by a potential vaccine. Among the sites the virus infects are cells of the immune system itself.

Much of the research has focused on understanding these roadblocks in the pathway to developing a successful preventive vaccine. An important breakthrough in our understanding of the mechanism of escape from the immune response to HIV came in 2012 and was published in the prestigious journal *Nature Medicine* by Professor Penny Moore and her colleagues of the NICD.[136] They demonstrated that the production of antibodies that would be broadly active against the constantly changing different antigens of the virus was delayed up to several years after initial infection. With the ever-evolving mutational changes in the structure of the crucial antigens on the surface of the virus, for a vaccine to be effective it would need to elicit broadly reactive neutralising antibodies.

Further studies by the CHIVSTI in subsequent years have provided answers to some of these critical questions regarding the evolution of HIV in infected individuals. However, the mechanisms of this evolution are still not fully understood, nor is there enough clarity on the route to develop a preventive vaccine capable of eliciting broadly reacting neutralising antibodies.

Could the body's immune system itself be educated into broadening its neutralising antibody response to react to and address the ever-evolving virus mutations?

Several observations have suggested that there may be a natural resistance to the virus. The question arises whether the mechanisms responsible for this natural resistance could offer clues as to what might be needed in a vaccine.

It was observed quite early in the epidemic that HIV infection resulted in a wide range of illnesses of varying virulence. Some individuals, unfortunately, experienced a galloping stormy course of the illness which quite rapidly led to death – these are called 'rapid progressors'. On the other end of the spectrum were HIV-infected individuals who would live relatively healthy lives, even without treatment, for many years – the so-called long-term non-progressors, now more correctly referred to as 'elite controllers'. What furnished the latter individuals with the ability to so effectively suppress the virus for so many years?

At the extreme end of the spectrum of resistance were individuals who seemed to be fully resistant to being infected with the virus, despite repeated exposures. The CHIVSTI has been studying a group of female sex workers who were resistant to infection with the virus. They had been in the profession for at least four years, averaging 17 different sexual partners per week, half of whom were HIV positive and uncommonly using condoms. And yet, despite this extraordinarily heavy exposure, these sex workers remained free of the virus. Preliminary studies revealed a possible explanation. There appear to be some individuals who are genetically deficient in auxiliary receptors for the virus, which are located on the surface of the cell and which the virus needs to gain entry into the cell.

Another observation that could possibly provide clues as to natural resistance to infection was the mother-to-infant model. Could the fact that the majority of infants born to HIV-positive mothers are not infected while in the womb offer important clues as to some intrinsic protective mechanism in most unborn infants which prevents them from being infected by the mother?

These observations have ignited intense research efforts searching for clues that could be of benefit in designing a future HIV preventive vaccine. These so-called natural experiments – that is, phenomena occurring in the natural world – have spawned important pointers and indicators for vaccine research.

In addition to its own extensive vaccine-related research, the CHIVSTI also provides key specialised laboratory support to the international HIV Vaccine Trials Network (HVTN), which is involved in clinical trials of candidate vaccines.

7

Vaccination and the eradication of disease

With the possible exception of the provision of clean water, no public health intervention has had a more profound effect on reducing sickness and death than vaccination. It is impossible to calculate, and difficult to estimate, the number of lives that have been saved by the routine administration of vaccines. The WHO has provided an estimate of four to five million deaths prevented each year because of vaccines.[137]

Another example of the power of vaccines comes from US data, showing that the number of cases and the number of deaths from the 10 most-feared epidemic and pandemic communicable diseases have been reduced by 96 to 100 per cent.[138] The picture is similar in all Western countries that have similar excellent public health systems.

A GOAL WITH THREE PHASES

The goal of overcoming communicable diseases – for example, through vaccination – can be divided into three progressively ambitious phases: control, elimination and eradication.[139]

Phase 1: Control

At the control stage, diseases have been successfully reduced in frequency to a low level; they are still present in the region or country but do not constitute a significant burden on the healthcare of the population. Control measures do still need to be in place to maintain that low level of disease. These measures include the continuing maintenance of the effective intervention which, in the case of vaccines, means achieving and retaining high levels of vaccine coverage. Importantly, competent monitoring is required to ensure that the disease continues to remain under control. Many vaccine-preventable diseases such as measles, whooping cough and diphtheria would fall into this category in South Africa.

Phase 2: Elimination

The elimination of a disease is defined by the total absence of that disease and the infective agent, in a region or a country, as a result of deliberate, active intervention. Protective measures are essential to ensure that the infective agent is not reintroduced from outside or re-established from any hidden internal source. In addition, to provide confidence and assurance that the infective agent is not present in that region, robust surveillance and monitoring programmes are crucial. Further, vaccination coverage needs to be maintained at a high level to ensure that the population's immunity remains sufficiently protective. In South Africa, polio would fall into this category.

Phase 3: Eradication

What is meant by eradication is the total removal of an infective agent throughout the world and, as a result, control measures are no longer necessary. Surveillance programmes can likewise be dispensed with. Eradication has only been achieved with two infectious organisms – smallpox in humans and rinderpest in ruminants, including cattle.

THE SUCCESSFUL ERADICATION OF SMALLPOX

Smallpox was one of the most formidable plagues of history, disfiguring or killing royalty, statesmen and commoners alike. The toll of smallpox in the twentieth century alone is estimated at 300 million dead.[140]

An iconic photo of a Somali chef named Ali Maow Maalin graces the walls of many public health offices across the world. He was the last person on earth known to have been naturally infected with the smallpox virus. The portrait triumphantly reflects the greatest victory of twentieth-century public health medicine: the total eradication of an infectious disease from the planet through vaccination. It also illustrates the extraordinary potential power of vaccines to control human infectious diseases. The success became the spur to bring other vaccine-preventable diseases into consideration for eradication.

The beginning of the end of smallpox – 1796

In 1796 an English country doctor named Edward Jenner inaugurated the first human vaccination in history by successfully vaccinating James Phipps, the eight-year-old son of his gardener. Some 200 years later the disease had been drastically reduced in most of the world and global authorities felt emboldened to embark on one of the most far-reaching public health campaigns of history – the global eradication of smallpox. The campaign was launched by the WHO in 1967 when smallpox was still responsible for some two million deaths annually.[141]

The campaign to eradicate smallpox consisted, essentially, of two components.[142] First was a mass campaign aiming at vaccinating 80 per cent of the world's population. This would involve vaccination teams reaching the most remote and inaccessible regions on the planet. In areas of conflict, 'days of tranquillity' were established where hostilities between warring sides were temporarily halted, enabling vaccination teams to enter those regions and do their life-saving work. The second phase was essentially a mopping-up programme, identifying remnant cases and then ring-vaccinating a wide circle of possible contacts of each identified case.

Why was smallpox targeted for eradication?

Many factors facilitated the success of the smallpox eradication campaign.

Firstly, the vaccine had an excellent track record demonstrating high efficacy in protecting individuals in much of the world. It was also easy to administer, even by relatively untrained workers and volunteers, by scratching it into the skin. The tell-tale scar where the vaccine had been administered was a readily visible sign of a person having been vaccinated and presumably signalled immunity to infection. A bonus, especially important in remote tropical regions, was the fact that the vaccine was also relatively heat stable and did not require the same cold-chain storage and transport conditions that applied to most other vaccines.

Secondly, the disease itself was easily recognisable, even by non-medically trained individuals, because of the characteristic clinical manifestation of disfiguring scarring that followed the blistering rash, which was especially visible on the face. This facilitated mop-up ring-vaccination of any contacts of infected individuals, thus preventing further spread.

Furthermore, individuals appeared to be contagious only once they developed the easily recognisable rash, particularly on the face, and could thus be timeously isolated.

Lastly, because the smallpox virus only affected humans, it provided reassurance that there would not be a reintroduction of the virus from an animal source once eradication was achieved.

The triumph of eradication

After a decade of intensive campaigning, the last naturally acquired case of smallpox was detected in 1977 in Merca, Somalia. On 8 May 1980 the formal document certifying the eradication of smallpox was signed at the WHO headquarters in Geneva.[143] The smallpox eradication campaign was estimated to have cost some US$300 million (an eighth of the cost of putting a man on the moon). On the benefits side, approximately US$1 000 million per annum will be saved in perpetuity by stopping smallpox vaccination and smallpox surveillance programmes.

Potential risks

As prized as eradication of a disease is, with its attendant saving of human lives and dispensing with the need for vaccination and surveillance programmes, there is one serious potential danger in the noble eradication goal. Eradicating a communicable disease also creates the theoretical threat of an unanticipated re-appearance of the eradicated agent, or closely related agent, into an increasingly susceptible population – and the spectre of a fertile opening for a biological weapon.

With the abolition of vaccination and natural infection, the global population progressively becomes more susceptible to the eradicated communicable disease agent should it somehow re-appear. There is therefore a critical need to be confident that there are no potential sources of the organism anywhere in the world. In addition, there would need to be assurances that the virus does not exist in any laboratory in the world other than in an absolute minimum number of facilities where it can be kept under very strictly maintained and regularly monitored security.

How safe is the world now from smallpox? The spectre of smallpox reintroduction has provided meat for several movie thrillers and books. The dangers have been documented in books such as *Scourge: The Once and Future Threat of Smallpox*, by Jonathan B. Tucker, and *Biohazard*, by Ken Alibek. Alibek (formerly Kanatzhan Alibekov) was a leader of the Soviet Union's bioweapons programme before he emigrated to the US. Both books highlight the spectre of the virus escaping from laboratories, either by accident or, as Alibek alludes to in his narrative, its deliberate exploitation as a bioweapon.

The fear of a laboratory escape became a reality in August 1978, less than a year after the last naturally occurring smallpox case in the world.[144] A 40-year-old medical photographer at the University of Birmingham in England, Mrs Janet Parker, contracted smallpox and died a month later – the last person in the world to die of smallpox. The inquiry into the incident found that she had probably been infected by virus aerosols in currents coursing through ducts from the microbiology laboratories on the floor below, where smallpox research was being carried out. (Professor Henry Bedson, the head of the microbiology department, subsequently committed suicide – his suicide note reading, 'I am sorry to have misplaced the trust which so many of my friends and colleagues have placed in me and my work.')

With the world's population becoming increasingly susceptible to smallpox following the cessation of vaccination, the fear of live smallpox virus escaping from a laboratory weighed heavily on the minds of global health authorities. The WHO campaigned vigorously for laboratories throughout the world to destroy any stocks of the virus they might have in their refrigerators. The goal was to have the virus stored in only two laboratories in the world: at the CDC in Atlanta in the US and at the Russian State Research Center of Virology and Biotechnology, in Novosibirsk. Following the Birmingham incident, laboratories throughout the world eagerly complied by destroying any remaining samples potentially containing the smallpox virus. But there was one exception that still held out and refused to destroy its stock – the NIV in South Africa. It was this lack of responsibility for the biosecurity of the world where the NIV was forced to play a 'spoiler' role in the early 1980s by holding onto samples of the eradicated smallpox virus after it had been eradicated globally.

The NIV and smallpox eradication

The destruction of smallpox samples in laboratories throughout the world was overseen by on-site inspection teams from the WHO. By the early 1980s, the drive to limit laboratory smallpox stocks was all but complete, except for the NIV in South Africa, which then became one of three laboratories in the world still holding onto the virus. Numerous pleadings from the WHO fell on the deaf ears of South Africa's Department of Health. Even the threat of cutting the last remaining thread of international scientific contact with the WHO failed to move the government. The reason given was that intelligence reports indicated that Cuban and East German troops, at the time in combat with the South African army in Angola and Namibia, were being vaccinated against smallpox. It was therefore deemed essential for the country to retain stocks of the smallpox virus.

Pressure from the scientific and medical community of South Africa, and especially from within the NIV itself, still failed to convince the authorities of the futility of this obstinacy. As was typical of the suspicious atmosphere and the secrecy of that era, on 10 December 1983 we were in for a surprise. As the staff of the institute were settling into their annual end-of-the-year party, without warning a message came through to me that the minister of health and a television crew were on their way to the NIV to destroy the last remaining South African stocks of smallpox! And so it came about that a small handful of NIV staff witnessed the minister of health pressing the button of the steriliser in the BSL-4 laboratory for the TV cameras to record the incineration of a few rusted tin vials labelled 'Smallpox Virus'. The WHO's *Weekly Epidemiological Record* of 23/30 December 1983 documented the destruction of the NIV's smallpox stocks, thereby certifying that the only remaining virus was securely stored under stringent biocontainment conditions in the US and Russia.

Subsequently, several of the annual meetings of the World Health Assembly featured debates between scientists unsuccessfully lobbying to destroy even the last two remaining stocks of the virus and, on the other side, scientists defending the retention of these stocks for current and future research. The debate continues to this day.

MONKEYPOX AND OTHER POXVIRUSES

Over and above the anxiety of a laboratory escape of smallpox virus, post-eradication there has also been a concern for the introduction of a poxvirus from an animal source, as could occur with human infection with a zoonotic poxvirus, which could occupy the vacant niche left by smallpox and potentially be responsible for a smallpox-type pandemic.[145]

The poxvirus family, technically called *Poxviridae*, is a large family of over 80 species, infecting creatures ranging from arthropods to vertebrates. Related to human smallpox are cowpox (which Jenner used as his vaccine against smallpox), camelpox, horsepox and monkeypox. Of these, the most interest has been centred on monkeypox, the only member of the poxvirus family known to cause potentially serious diseases in humans.

Monkeypox virus was first isolated in 1958, some two decades before the final eradication of smallpox. The name 'monkeypox' is misleading as the main animal reservoir of the virus is not monkeys, but rather small mammals, such as squirrels, rats and mice. The name arose after the virus was first isolated from laboratory monkeys in Denmark, and the name 'monkey' stuck. (Efforts are now being made by the WHO to change the name to avoid any disparaging African connotation.)

The first human case of monkeypox was identified in 1970 in the DRC.[146] The virus, currently endemic in 11 African countries, appears as two distinct strains – a West African strain and a Congo Basin strain. The disease seems to be less severe than smallpox, which it resembles clinically, with the mortality in endemic countries being approximately three to six per cent. The West African strain appears to be less severe. On occasion, sporadic cases have been imported into several non-endemic countries, chiefly by travellers from endemic regions.

In December 2003, a small, contained outbreak of monkeypox occurred in pet prairie dogs in the US. These dogs were imported from Ghana and were infected by rodents which shared the same housing. The outbreak involved some 70 individuals but did not cause severe disease.

Global outbreak 2022

The global monkeypox outbreak began in early May 2022. Following the introduction of the virus, it spread rapidly and, as of 15 September of that year, 61 282 cases had been confirmed in 96 countries throughout the world, with 20 deaths, half of them in non-endemic countries.[147]

On 23 July 2022, the WHO declared the outbreak to be a Public Health Emergency of International Concern, a proclamation which empowers international health authorities with appropriate instruments to help control and stamp out an outbreak.

It became clear that the virus had seeded itself into the social networks of the MSM (men who have sex with men) community globally. Some 98 per cent of cases were reported in young men identifying themselves as MSM or bisexual, of which 41 per cent were reported in individuals living with HIV – which may have further facilitated the spread of the virus.

The disease closely resembles smallpox, with the elements of the characteristic rash being very similar. As with smallpox, the blisters and pustules are heavily laden with virus particles. Transmission occurs as a result of skin-to-skin contact.

Because the two viruses are similar, the smallpox vaccine is effective in protecting against monkeypox. However, with the cessation of smallpox vaccination some 50 years previously, the majority of the human population has never experienced the smallpox vaccine. Even in the older population who had been vaccinated there is a significant waning of protective immunity. Modifications of the original smallpox vaccine, to render it safer and more effective, are currently being used in monkeypox vaccination programmes and the outbreak does appear to be declining worldwide.

Much still needs to be learned about monkeypox. The infection is of relatively low transmissibility because of the mode of spread, with little or no spread via the respiratory route before the onset of recognisable clinical symptoms such as the rash. Was the rapid worldwide spread merely due to the unfortunate introduction, and subsequent seeding, into the widely connected global MSM social network? Or, more ominously, could there have been a change in the virus's genetic structure with mutational changes facilitating its transmissibility?[148] The latter question needs urgently to be addressed as other animal poxviruses wait menacingly in the wings.

THE GLOBAL ERADICATION OF POLIO

Before the advent of routine vaccination, polio was one of the most feared diseases in the Western world. With the introduction of the Salk inject-able vaccine in the latter half of the 1950s and the Sabin oral polio vaccine in the 1960s, the number of polio cases fell dramatically. In the US, for instance, the epidemic was rapidly reduced to fewer than 100 cases in the 1960s and less than 10 in the 1970s.

In 1979 polio was eliminated from the US. On occasion a case was brought in by travellers, but with widespread vaccination any potential spread was rapidly stamped out. The story was similar in all developed countries.

The power of the polio vaccine dramatically to control the infection, combined with the conquest of smallpox, gave global health planners the incentive and the drive to plan for the next eradication campaign.

The WHO Global Polio Eradication Initiative (GPEI)

Within a decade of the triumphant eradication of smallpox, a programme to eradicate, through surveillance and vaccination, the second human commu-nicable disease – poliomyelitis – was inaugurated. Unfortunately, it would turn out to be a vastly more difficult challenge than eradicating smallpox.

On 27 May 1988, the *Weekly Epidemiological Record* of the WHO published the announcement, from the 41st World Health Assembly, of a programme to eradicate polio from the planet by the year 2000. The programme, which was to be known as the Global Polio Eradication Initiative (GPEI), was a public-private partnership of several national governments together with six partners – the WHO, Rotary International, the CDC, UNICEF (the United Nations Children's Fund), the Bill and Melinda Gates Foundation, and the GAVI vaccine alliance (Global Alliance for Vaccines and Immunization).

Similarities and challenges

There were indeed several similarities between the two diseases but, unfortunately, also some important differences that turned out to be for-midable challenges.

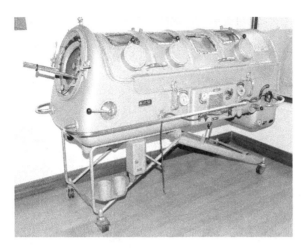

Figure 1:   The iron lung – a relic of the polio outbreaks before the advent of the polio vaccine. The iron lung was a machine in which unfortunate victims of paralytic poliomyelitis, unable to breathe as a result of the paralysis of the muscles of respiration, were more or less permanently encased. The individual was placed inside the central chamber of the machine, which had a door to allow the head and neck to remain free. The rest of the chamber was sealed, forming an airtight compartment. Pumps controlled the airflow to the lungs by cyclically decreasing and increasing the air pressure within the chamber and, particularly, on the chest wall. In this way, the iron lung artificially replaced the paralysed respiratory muscles. The advent of the enormously successful polio vaccine saw the rapid demise of the iron lung. Photograph by Guy Hall.

Figure 2:   The iconic picture of Ali Maow Maalin – the last human to have been naturally infected with smallpox, October 1977, in Merca, Somalia. Ali, being scared of needles, avoided being vaccinated. He contracted the minor form of the disease and recovered fully. While he was the last naturally infected case, the final victim of smallpox was a laboratory technologist, Janet Parker, accidentally infected as a result of a laboratory accident at the University of Birmingham. She died of smallpox in September 1978. On 9 December 1979, the WHO officially declared the infection to have been eradicated from the planet. © World Health Organization/John Wickett, 1979.

Figure 3: Following the eradication of smallpox, Ali Maow Maalin devoted his energies to promoting polio vaccination in Somalia and became a WHO district officer for the Global Polio Eradication Initiative. He famously said: 'Somalia was the last country with smallpox. I wanted to ensure that we would not be the last place with polio too.' Sadly, on 22 July 2013, at the age of 59, Ali passed away from malaria in his home district of Merca. © World Health Organization/Edna Adan Ismail, 1988.

Figure 4: The Centre for Tuberculosis is housed in a purpose-built construction which was completed in 2009 and is the most recent building on the NICD campus. Because of the biohazardous nature of the activities in these laboratories, the building is designed with minimal openings to the outside. The walls on three sides of the building are comprised of pre-cast concrete blocks which are perforated by apertures for natural light and are conceived to resemble the pattern seen when sequencing the DNA of an organism, such as TB. Photograph by Guy Hall.

Figure 5: The NICD has built four highly specialised structures to carry out research on medically important mosquitoes. These insectaries are purpose-built constructions specifically to breed mosquitoes. At the NICD they are predominantly used to investigate and carry out research related to malaria. The walls of these singular buildings consist of specially insulated panelling to enable the maintenance of climate control at 25 degrees Celsius. In addition, unlike regular constructions based on concrete, these panels need to be resistant to the continuous humidity of 80 per cent. Photograph by Guy Hall.

Figure 6: A mosquito-handling laboratory inside one of the four insectaries of the NICD. Mosquito colonies are bred from specimens collected in the field and are used to investigate their ability to carry and transmit pathogenic organisms such as malaria. In order to successfully breed mosquitoes, these laboratories are maintained at a constant temperature of 25 degrees Celsius and a humidity of 80 per cent. The lights are programmed on a 12/12 hour day/night lighting cycle with dusk and dawn transitions, to mimic conditions in nature. Photograph by Guy Hall.

Figure 7: Wastewater surveillance. A technician from the NICD Wastewater Genomics Syndicate takes a sample of wastewater through a maintenance hole which provides access to the pipes conveying sewage to the treatment plants. As the virus is excreted in stool, testing of wastewater is a powerful diagnostic tool and an important component of surveillance for Covid-19. Wastewater surveillance has become a particularly valuable diagnostic tool as it provides information about organisms, including pathogens, circulating in a whole community serviced by that sewage system, as against surveillance based on individual clinical specimens. Photograph by Tshepiso Seleka.

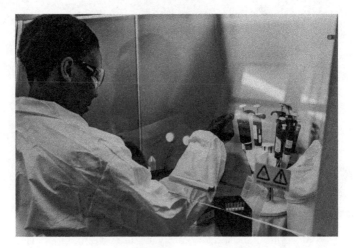

Figure 8: Wastewater samples are examined by the PCR test for the presence of SARS-CoV-2. As the PCR test is exquisitely sensitive because of the multiple rounds of amplification, it is able to detect minute amounts of the virus's RNA even when it is diluted in a large volume of wastewater. The amplified RNA of the virus can then be further examined by sequencing the genome to look out for a new variant or subvariant. Photograph by Tshepiso Seleka.

Figure 9: From 1999 to 2005, the Treatment Action Campaign, founded by Zackie Achmat and others, led civil society activism in tackling the tragic HIV/AIDS denial stance of the South African government. In this picture Zackie Achmat is seen confronting the then minister of health, Manto Tshabalala-Msimang, concerning the government's delay in rolling out desperately needed antiretroviral drug treatment. Photograph by David Goldblatt.

Figure 10: On 28 May 2021, the federal minister of health of Germany, Jens Spahn, visited the NICD labs with the South African minister of health, Dr Zweli Mkhize, on the occasion of the handover of a state-of-the-art Cobus 8800 machine. This machine automates the diagnostic PCR test and was used extensively for SARS-CoV-2 diagnosis. From left to right: Ms Rivashni Madho (scientist in the molecular laboratory), Professor Adrian Puren (NICD director), Jens Spahn and Dr Zweli Mkhize. Photograph by Christoph Soeder.

Figure 11: The hammer-headed fruit bat (*Hypsignathus monstrosus*) is the largest bat on the African continent, with a wingspan of up to three feet (91 cm) and is widely distributed in tropical West and Central Africa. This species of bat is of concern as a potential reservoir host for the Ebola virus. Although the natural reservoir of Ebola has yet to be established, interest in the hammer-headed bat has been sparked by the finding of antibodies to the virus, and even viral nucleic acid sequences, in these animals by NICD investigators during the Ebola outbreaks in the Democratic Republic of the Congo. Available at https://journals.plos.org/plosone/article?id=10.1371/journal.pone.0223139

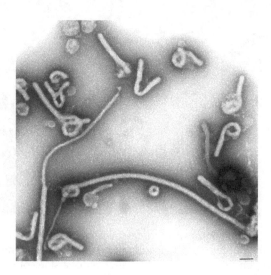

Figure 12: The dreaded Ebola virus visualised under the electron microscope appears as bizarre long filamentous structures. Scale bar on lower right = 100 nm (nanometres), or 100 millionth of an mm. Electron photo micrograph, Monica Birkhead.

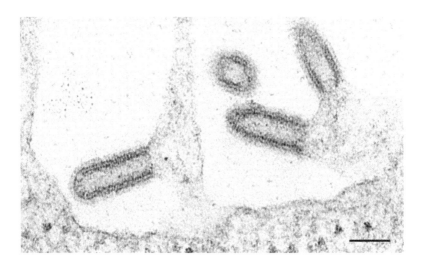

Figure 13: Rabies virus. The most lethal of all infectious organisms is characteristically recognised under the electron microscope as bullet-shaped virus particles, rounded at one end and flat on the other. In this image of the closely related, lookalike vesicular stomatitis virus, several of these bullet-shaped particles can be seen. Scale bar on lower right = 100 nm (nanometres), or 100 millionth of an mm. Electron photo micrograph, Monica Birkhead.

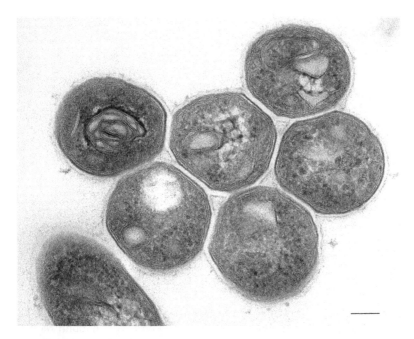

Figure 14: A group of tuberculosis bacteria (*Mycobacterium tuberculosis*) under the electron microscope. The cells of the bacteria are sectioned to display the complex internal structures (unlike the very much smaller and simpler structure of all viruses). Scale bar on lower right = 100 nm (nanometres), or 100 millionth of an mm. Electron photo micrograph, Monica Birkhead.

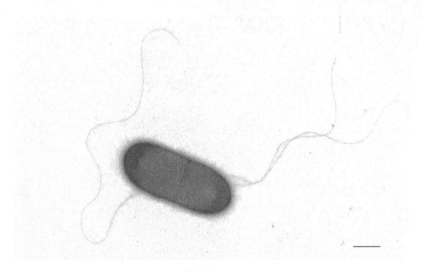

Figure 15: A *Listeria monocytogenes* bacterial cell seen under the electron microscope. A few of its typical whip-like appendices, called flagella, are clearly visible. Scale bar on lower right = 500 nm (nanometres), or 500 millionth of an mm. Electron photo micrograph, Monica Birkhead.

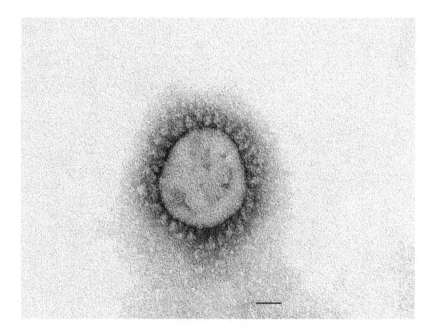

Figure 16: Electron microscopic image of SARS-CoV-2 virus – the causative agent of Covid-19. The spherical-shaped virus is enrobed with round knob-like protuberances which give the virus the appearance of a coronet – hence the name 'coronaviruses' for this family of viruses. Located in these protruding knobs are structures which enable the virus to attach to specific receptor sites on the surface of the cell. Scale bar below the image = 25 nm (nanometres), or 25 millionth of an mm. Electron photo micrograph, Monica Birkhead.

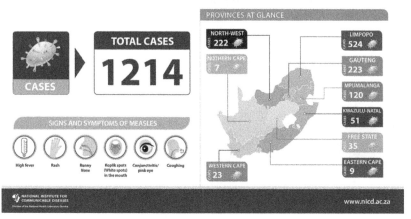

Figure 17:   A public health message distributed by the NICD regarding the recent measles outbreak in South Africa. Communication of relevant, accessible, scientifically based information to health professionals and the general public is a major responsibility of the NICD. Regular bulletins, communiqués, email messaging and an attractive website are the tools used to keep the public informed and updated on outbreaks and to disseminate important preventive messages. Infographic, Adrian J. Puren.

As with the smallpox vaccine, polio vaccines were also demonstrated to be extremely effective in protecting against infection. Similarly, the oral polio vaccine could also be administered by non-professional personnel. A further similarity, critical to the planning of eradication, was that polio infects only humans, giving comfort that there would not be a reintroduction from an animal source once eradication had been achieved. However, that was essentially where the similarities ended. The differences would prove to make polio eradication a far more daunting undertaking.

Unlike the smallpox vaccine, the polio vaccine is not heat stable and requires a well-maintained cold chain for storage and transport. As mentioned above, surveillance of smallpox was reasonably straightforward because of the high visibility of the easily recognisable clinical features of the rash, especially on the face. In addition the tell-tale vaccination scar facilitated surveillance of who had been vaccinated.

With polio, the challenge of finding individuals who were infected was far tougher. Some 70 per cent of those infected with the poliovirus had no symptoms at all; 29 per cent had non-specific symptoms, usually passed off as flu or gastroenteritis. In reality, only one per cent of those infected would demonstrate the recognisable clinical manifestation of polio – the characteristic flaccid paralysis. It would be down to looking for cases of acute flaccid paralysis (AFP) that became the major surveillance tool in the search for the remaining polio cases in the world.

Furthermore, control of smallpox had the major advantage that transmission of the virus was not particularly high and would only occur when the patient was aware of being infected. In other words, the characteristic rash made finding cases quite straightforward, and then control for spread by vaccination was very effective. Not so with polio. A case of AFP meant that up to a hundred times more unrecognised individuals in that vicinity would also be infected and possibly transmit the virus. The response to the detection of an AFP case was therefore mass vaccination over a wide range of possible contacts – often the entire country.[149] Important additional tools were also brought in to facilitate surveillance, such as sampling wastewater in sewage plants as the virus is excreted in stool.

The NIV, and later the NICD, with its rich history in polio research, played a crucial role in surveillance programmes for poliovirus on the African continent. The WHO regional reference laboratory for characterising polio strains at the NICD became an important centre for training scientists and public health workers from all over Africa and beyond.

Successes and setbacks

The first 15 years of the GPEI met with gratifying success. In 1988, when the initiative was launched, over 350 000 cases of paralytic polio were identified in some 125 endemic countries. By 2003, the number of polio cases in the world had shrunk down to 732 in six remaining endemic countries. Unfortunately, fortunes changed in 2003, and polio came back again! It spread to an additional 17 countries with a corresponding disheartening increase in cases. And so began the sober realisation that polio eradication was not so straightforward as originally contemplated when the initiative was first launched.[150]

It soon became clear that there were two daunting obstacles – a socio-political one and a vaccine virus one – standing in the way of reaching the elusive goal of eradication.[151]

A crucial ingredient to the success of any eradication programme is the acceptance and support of the community. With smallpox, buy-in from communities was driven both by the dread of the disfiguring clinical manifestations and significant mortality, as well as the well-recognised success of the vaccine. Community support stretched even as far as organising 'days of tranquillity' in conflict areas to allow for vaccination to take place. Lamentably, the human climate changed markedly in the ensuing few decades. The rise and influence of religious fundamentalism and its incendiary mix with global terrorism severely damaged the polio eradication campaign. Religious opposition to vaccination became widespread in India, Pakistan, Afghanistan and northern Nigeria, and children were hidden away from the vaccination teams. Suspicion of the West was accentuated by allegations that the CIA had organised a fake vaccination drive in Pakistan in 2011 to acquire DNA samples from the family of Osama bin Laden, in preparation for his assassination. Far from the welcoming milieu of the smallpox campaigns, polio vaccination teams were met with hostility and even violence. Dozens of polio vaccination workers were murdered by extremists in Pakistan, Afghanistan and, to a lesser extent, Nigeria. This was a far cry from the days of tranquillity of the smallpox campaign.

A second major obstacle to eradication came, ironically, from the oral polio vaccine itself. As mentioned, there are two kinds of polio vaccine: the injected vaccine (Salk vaccine) and the oral vaccine (Sabin vaccine). The injected vaccine is made by killing (inactivating) the poliovirus; the remaining protein structure then immunises the vaccine recipient. Being a killed vaccine, the vaccine virus cannot multiply. The oral vaccine, on the other hand, uses live poliovirus which has been modified (attenuated) to not cause disease. Being alive, it needs to multiply to a limited extent in the gut of the vaccine recipient to effectively stimulate the immune system. However, being a live virus, it does undergo mutations in the gut of the vaccine recipient, and it can potentially, in rare cases, regain the ability to cause polio disease, specifically paralysis. This mutant form of the oral vaccine poliovirus which regains the ability to spread and also the ability to cause paralysis is termed cVDPV (circulating Vaccine-Derived Poliovirus).[152] Today the majority of cases of paralytic polio in the world are isolated cases or even small outbreaks of cVDPV. These cases occur in unvaccinated individuals or populations where there is a low level of vaccine coverage. Because of the potential risk of cVDPV, most Western countries have now abandoned the oral polio vaccine and are vaccinating exclusively with the injected vaccine.

'Can polio be eradicated?' is a question that has been asked by many public health authorities, many of whom have advocated for a control strategy rather than an eradication one.[153] The initial deadline of 2000 came and went without eradication. Similarly, the next target date, 2005, from Rotary International (to mark the centenary of the establishment of their first club) also came and went. The Polio Endgame Strategy of 2019–2023 has now been replaced by a new Polio Eradication Strategy for 2022–2026.

Notwithstanding these setbacks, the eradication campaign has made enormous strides, even though eradication has yet to be achieved. The incidence of polio globally has dropped by 99.9 per cent, and approximately 16 million individuals are walking today who would otherwise have been paralysed, while over 1.5 million lives have been saved. Of the three types of polio in nature, type 2 and type 3 have already been eradicated, in 2015 and 2019 respectively. It is only type 1 that still exists in the world – some 18 cases in 2022 up to July of that year. More cases of paralytic polio due to cVDPV were recorded for 2022 – 187 up to mid July, including a case in New York State in an unvaccinated young man.[154]

Polio eradication is so tantalisingly, yet frustratingly, close to finality. The campaign needs to counter the despondency that may come from the recurring postponements of the target dates. Mobilisation of civil society and mobilisation of public opinion would also go some way to counter the fatigue felt at various levels, from healthcare worker and volunteer fatigue to donor fatigue; the last mentioned especially when considering competing, far more prominent health priorities.[155] Parental and community resistance requires grassroots mobilisation and peer communication. Dr Margaret Chan, director general of the WHO from 2006 to 2017, in her acceptance speech on 9 November 2006, at the height of the eradication setbacks, pledged '. . . we will complete polio eradication'.

The last mile in the marathon is always the hardest. Despite the setbacks, the GPEI will continue until it reaches its goal of wiping polio from the face of the earth.[156] But will there be attempts to eradicate further communicable diseases?

ERADICATION OF DISEASE – IS IT STILL A POSSIBILITY?

Eradication: feasibility and risks

The eminent Australian virologist Frank Fenner (1914–2010), who played a key role in the eradication of smallpox and announced to the World

Health Assembly in 1980 that smallpox had finally been eradicated, famously joined several prominent scientists, including a number of the pioneers of polio research, in arguing that the eradication of smallpox was a fortuitous one-off achievement, never to be repeated.[157] Consequently, to attempt to eradicate any other disease would be futile. Their proposal for polio was rather to accept indefinite vaccination for effective control and tolerate up to 500 cases per year globally.[158]

The biological argument, also known as the niche replacement hypothesis, warned that eradication may possibly have unintended consequences.[159] The argument is founded on the notion that pathogenic organisms occupy specific ecological niches in nature and related organisms compete with one another for shared resources within these niches. In other words, a related competitor organism could simply replace an eradicated organism in their shared niche. This was a real concern in the earlier days of the polio eradication campaign – the fear that the poliovirus, once eradicated, could be replaced by a non-polio enterovirus (specifically, by a member of the C-cluster of coxsackie A viruses).[160] The latter virus is also a recognised cause of AFP and may have a similar mode of spread.

Fortunately, this fear has not been realised. The recent 'revival' of the non-endemic monkeypox virus, as detailed above, was postulated to be the result of niche replacement following the smallpox eradication. Fortunately, there is currently no biological evidence for this and the vacant niche hypothesis has garnered little scientific support at the moment.

The International Task Force for Eradication

To strengthen eradication efforts, an International Task Force for Eradication was established in the US the same year that the polio eradication campaign was announced by the WHO in 1988.[161] Criteria for disease eradication were established and several diseases, including measles as well as others, were proposed for eradication. At present, there are two diseases actively on WHO eradication programmes – polio and

Guinea-worm disease. Both diseases are now far past their original target dates for eradication – 2000 for polio and 1986 for Guinea-worm. The scientific name for the latter disease is Dracunculiasis. It is a parasitic worm disease, still endemic in a few countries in Africa, the prevention of which rests on the provision of safe, clean drinking water.

The setbacks to the polio eradication campaign have demonstrated that, essentially, the single remaining obstacle is the buy-in and support for the campaign by the peoples of the world.[162]

The resounding success of the smallpox eradication campaign encouragingly demonstrated that a communicable disease agent can be totally eradicated from the world in perpetuity and with it the removal of further concerns for that disease or the means to control it. The final achievement represents the pinnacle of preventive medicine and the zenith of public health service to humankind.

Vaccines convincingly have the power to eradicate human disease, but it is the will of the people that is required to ensure success.

CHAPTER

8

Epidemics, pandemics and new communicable diseases

In early 2020 the world awoke to a rapidly unfolding health crisis more severe than anything seen since the devastating Spanish influenza pandemic of 1918/1919 which claimed some 50 million lives. Despite vastly more sophisticated health systems, the Covid pandemic was still able to overwhelm first-world health systems and claim at least seven million deaths. It almost brought many of the world's economies to their knees. The medical-scientific community, no less than the general public, were stunned by this unanticipated pandemic caused by a virus completely new to humankind. Many questions still remain to be answered, not least the still unsolved question of whether the virus arose naturally following spillover from the animal world – in other words, a zoonotic disease – or whether it was a leak from a laboratory housing or experimenting with the virus. These are intensely important issues and they require urgent answers if we are to anticipate and adequately prepare for future similar new infections of humankind. New infectious diseases will undoubtedly appear in the future as humans maintain their contact with exotic animals and their ecosystems or continue to be less meticulous with laboratory safety.

From biblical times to the present, plagues, epidemics and pandemics have played a major role in influencing the course of human history. And yet, if medical science has largely controlled, eliminated and even eradicated many of these diseases, why are we facing more and more previously unheard-of new infectious diseases? Are they genuinely 'new', or are we just getting better at picking more of them up with our far more advanced scientifically sophisticated tools?

Public health institutions such as the NICD are equipped with increasingly sophisticated, powerful and technologically advanced tools to detect pathogenic organisms. Diagnoses are without doubt much more precise, rapid and accurate than even a decade ago. Advanced technology strikingly demonstrated its prowess in January 2020 by discovering the causative agent of the new disease of Covid, the novel coronavirus, SARS-CoV-2, within a week of recognising the clinical illness.[163] It soon also established that SARS-CoV-2 was a genuinely new infection of humans and, as is the case with the great majority of truly new communicable diseases, originated from animal sources (zoonotic diseases).[164]

The concept of 'newness' is sometimes used loosely, not necessarily always to denote a genuine new infection to humankind. It is also sometimes used to refer to communicable diseases that may be new to a region as a result of importation, such as we saw with monkeypox being introduced into the Western world from its endemic home in Africa. 'Newness' is also used to refer to those diseases that have re-appeared after being absent for many years, such as we saw with the polio case in New York State, which was the first case since 2013 in the United States. In these cases these diseases are, of course, not new to humankind.

THE INTRODUCTION OF 'NEW' DISEASES TO HUMANS

Epidemics and pandemics (the worldwide spread of an epidemic) of new diseases arise in two stages: firstly, the zoonotic spillover event introduces the infectious organism, in the main a virus, into the human population from an animal source. The second stage involves various factors that could promote the widespread dissemination of the pathogenic communicable organism throughout the human population,

Zoonotic spillover

A spillover event occurs when a communicable disease agent crosses the species barrier from animals to humans and then gets established in the human population.[165] This may be the result of humans intruding into remote isolated wild animal ecosystems, or, alternately, when wild animals are driven to venture into human habitats or are purposely brought into human environments .

Alien animal viruses entering the human biome

The successful introduction of an alien animal virus into the human population is a rare event. Why this is rare is because of the need for the virus to attach itself to a very specific receptor site on the cell's surface to initiate infection. The attachment to the receptor site is highly specific to that virus in much the same way as a key fits a lock. On that rare occasion when the key can fit the lock, the invading virus successfully establishes itself in the host cell and then initiates the infection process.

Inside the cell the virus replicates itself using the machinery of the cell. The progeny virus is released from the cell only to infect further cells and repeat the replication process. The next step is for it to be released from the body to infect another individual and establish a chain of transmission from human to human, which could ultimately lead to an outbreak of a communicable disease.

The behaviour of modern humankind has played a large part in the advent of these new communicable diseases. The increasing wildlife trading of exotic animals worldwide, both legal and illegal, facilitates an ever-growing wild animal-human interaction. Multiple opportunities for these interactions to take place result from the trade of exotic animals, or as a result of agricultural expansion and deforestation of wildlife habitats, or the preparation and consumption of wild animals for food in the so-called wet markets of the Far East. The most prominent and widely recognised example of the last mentioned is the events that took place at the Huanan Seafood Wholesale Market in Wuhan, China, which led up to the Covid-19 pandemic of today – to be discussed later.

The reverse chain of events may occur when wild animals are driven to move out of their established habitats and into those of humans in search of food.

Climate change and new infections

Climate change has emerged as one of the most serious threats to human health – from floods to droughts to extremes of temperature. Climate change also poses a serious indirect threat to human health as a result of habitat destruction and its knock-on effect on communicable diseases in humans. The outbreak of the viral disease Nipah in Malaysia and Singapore in 1998/1999 provides a graphic example of how the combination of environmental destruction together with climate change can create the ingredients for new human diseases. The Nipah virus outbreak involved 276 cases, 106 of them fatal.[166] The natural host of this virus is the fruit bat which lives in the forests of these two countries. A combination of the climatic effect of drought, due to the El Niño event,[167] together with a human element – massive deforestation by large-scale burning of vegetation – created a severe haze, which reduced the flowering and fruiting of forest trees. Deprived of their natural food source, the fruit bats invaded the cultivated orchards and transmitted the virus to domestic pigs who, in turn, infected humans. The outbreak was brought under control by the large-scale slaughtering of the local pig population.

Once a new communicable disease is established in the human population, the next stage for it to progress to a new epidemic or pandemic depends on factors that promote its spread. It is the route of transmission of the infection that largely determines the extent and the speed of the resulting outbreak. For example, organisms that spread through the gastrointestinal route – that is, by ingestion of faecal-contaminated food or water – may spread widely and quite rapidly, as was the case with the cholera pandemics of the past, but are limited to geographic areas poorly supplied with clean water. The key to preventing such outbreaks is largely the provision of clean water.

Far more difficult to prevent and control are organisms that are transmitted via the respiratory route, because the communicable organism is disseminated through the air we breathe. The risk is further magnified if the organism is spread before the person becomes ill, or where it does not cause clinical symptoms and the individual may be unaware of being infected and infectious. Those respiratory-spread diseases that are communicable only while the patient is clinically ill may be a lot easier to control, as they would be easier to recognise as being a potential source of infection and the patient can be isolated from other individuals to avoid transmitting the infection. The original SARS outbreak of 2003 caused by the related SARS-CoV-1 virus was thus much easier to control than the current SARS-CoV-2 outbreak, where most transmission occurs from individuals who are not aware of being infected, either because they have no symptoms or before symptoms develop.[168] The plagues of antiquity moved slowly because in those days transportation was far slower. In contrast, with modern air travel plagues can now be very easily transmitted from one end of the world to the other within a day or two.

In summary, we should not be too surprised that the twenty-first century has presented us with a number of new communicable diseases. Human-wild animal interactions have been promoted by human activities seriously damaging the natural environment of the planet.

Finally, humans of the twenty-first century are challenged by these new diseases in much the same way as the Native Americans of the fifteenth and sixteenth centuries, who suffered massive population losses from 'new' communicable agents brought to their shores by colonising Europeans.[169] In these so-called virgin soil epidemics the novel organism, being completely new to the population, encounters no resistance from population immunity and is therefore able to spread virtually unhindered.

Most new infections have been able to be contained and prevented from causing widespread epidemics. In many of them, their mode of transmission does not facilitate extensive spread. For example, the transmission of Ebola and Marburg virus depends on close contact with blood and blood-containing secretions.[170] Widespread outbreaks have occurred in limited geographic areas deprived of adequate sanitary facilities. Where sporadic cases have been imported into developed countries, modern hygienic practices and resources have prevented them from spreading further.

We now need to look at the rather chilling word 'pandemic'. In its broadest sense, it means a disease that affects large parts of the world, or even the entire world. Communicable diseases such as HIV/AIDS could fit into this definition. However, the word 'pandemic' would more usually be used to refer to an acute communicable disease that is sudden in onset and spreads rapidly over very large areas of the world. A number of communicable diseases of antiquity, such as smallpox, plague (the Black Death), cholera, measles and others, could well fall into this definition of pandemic. Most of these have now been eliminated or controlled by public health measures, vaccines and the provision of clean water. In more modern times, there are two communicable diseases that stand out as paradigms of pandemics – influenza and Covid-19.

THE INFLUENZA PANDEMICS

The mother of all pandemics, the Spanish influenza pandemic of 1918/1919, swept through the world in three waves towards the close of the Great War. The virus is estimated to have infected a third of the world's population, killing up to 50 million people, overtaking the estimated 25 million people who died in the Black Death of the Middle Ages. South Africa was severely affected, losing six per cent of its entire population in a matter of six weeks.[171]

Genetic instability of the influenza virus

In 1933, the influenza virus was one of the first human viruses isolated, and yet it still remains one of the most enigmatic.[172] Its ability to continually change its surface protein (the haemagglutinin) responsible for attaching the virus to its specific receptor site on the cell it infects is referred to as 'antigenic drift'. This characteristic property of the virus allows it continually to escape the host's immunity, thereby ensuring that it will be an unwelcome guest every winter season. The annual bouts of seasonal influenza are estimated to be responsible for approximately 400 000 respiratory deaths globally.[173]

Because of antigenic drift, the annual influenza vaccine needs to be updated every year to match the strains incorporated into the vaccine to those circulating in the community. As mentioned in Chapter 4, one of the important responsibilities of the influenza laboratory of the NICD is to track the antigenic drift in order to provide currently circulating isolates of the virus to the WHO, who, in turn, distribute stock strains of the annually updated virus to vaccine manufacturers.

A more profound change in the virus occurs as a result of genetic fragments being swapped between different strains of the virus during their replication when they happen simultaneously to infect the same cell. This results in a much more profound antigenic change (antigenic shift). Fortunately, this is far less common, occurring approximately two to three times a century. It was this process that was responsible for the pandemics of influenza in 1889/1890, 1899/1900, 1918/1919 (Spanish influenza), 1957/1958 (Asian flu), and 1968/1969 (Hong Kong flu). The major reservoir of the influenza virus is birds (avian influenza), and zoonotic infections originating in birds may well be the source of the novel antigenic material that may occasionally enter the human population through the mechanism of antigenic shift, resulting in substantially different new strains against which humans would have little immunity. It is these radically new strains that are responsible for the rare but serious global influenza pandemics that occur a few times each century.

The threat of avian influenza

Avian influenza is the most-feared communicable disease in the poultry industry worldwide. The 2004/2005 outbreak was estimated by the Food and Agricultural Organization (FAO), a specialised agency of the UN, to have resulted in the death or destruction of over 200 million birds worldwide, at a cost of over US$200 billion.[174] In South Africa, the ostrich industry was decimated by the 2004 avian influenza outbreak, with over 2 000 birds killed in three weeks.[175]

In 2005 zoonotic spillover to humans, particularly to workers in close contact with infected birds, resulted in some 628 cases of avian influenza, 374 of them fatal, in 15 countries. Given this exceptionally high mortality rate, there was a great deal of international alarm should avian influenza entrench itself in the human population and be responsible for a new worldwide pandemic. Pandemic preparedness plans were drawn up by many countries throughout the world and by the WHO. My esteemed colleague Professor Salim Abdool Karim, from the Centre for the AIDS Programme of Research in South Africa (CAPRISA) in KwaZulu-Natal, and I drew up an Emergency Plan for South Africa to prepare for any future pandemic influenza threat.

The Spanish influenza pandemic

The earlier phases of the 1918/1919 Spanish flu pandemic were predominantly seen in the population of decommissioned servicemen. Pitiful reports were recorded of fit and ostensibly healthy young servicemen falling down on the parade ground and dying the same day. Similar accounts of rapidly fatal illnesses were recorded in civilian populations, often in people of a young age. Why the influenza of that pandemic was so lethal still remains a mystery. The virus itself is of course no longer available for study. However, modern technologies such as the PCR – polymerase chain reaction – have enabled researchers to amplify surviving genetic material from the virus to look for clues in specific genetic sequences to try to explain the apparent extreme virulence of the virus.[176] PCR is an exquisitely sensitive technique used in the laboratory to very rapidly amplify a specific segment of the genome to produce millions of copies, thus enabling the segment to be identified and studied.

In the case of Spanish flu, material was obtained for PCR from the bodies of individuals who died of the disease and were buried in permafrost – for example, in an Inuit community in Brevig Mission, Alaska. Tissue embedded in paraffin blocks that had been kept for examination in pathology laboratories in the US from the pandemic were also investigated for any remnants of the virus. However, numerous studies have still failed to identify any specific genetic signature for the profound virulence.[177]

Attention then turned to interrogating the social circumstances at the time for clues, especially the circumstances surrounding demobilised servicemen at the end of the Great War. Unfortunately, no specific indicators could be identified. Perhaps even more perplexing is that the virus (subtype H1N1), soon after the pandemic abated, took its place as a relatively mild cause of seasonal influenza illness, and still circulates widely in humans.

A century later, humanity would again be challenged with a respiratory virus causing a similar illness. But this time, unlike the unsophisticated public health and medical practices of the early twentieth century, the new pandemic, Covid-19, would be met with the advanced biomedical science of the twenty-first century.

THE COVID-19 PANDEMIC

The Covid-19 pandemic, the first major pandemic since the Spanish influenza pandemic a century previously, also claimed a heavy toll on human lives. As of 31 May 2023, just under seven million people were reported to have died of the infection, although the true mortality figure may well be two to three times higher because of under-reporting.[178] Both the influenza and the coronavirus pandemics are primarily respiratory diseases, spread between individuals through virus-laden fluid aerosols inhaled into the respiratory tract. Not surprisingly, restrictions and mask mandates imposed during the Covid-19 pandemic also markedly reduced the incidence of seasonal influenza.[179] However, in many other respects, the Covid-19 pandemic of the early twenty-first century was quite different to the influenza pandemic of the early twentieth century, not least because of the gift of scientific progress over the last century.

A pandemic in the era of twenty-first-century technology

Within weeks after Chinese health authorities became aware of a cluster of unusual cases of pneumonia in Wuhan, central China, in late 2019, the virus was isolated and grown, and merely a week later, the genome – that is, the total genetic information of an organism, or the repository of information to code for the structure and function of the organism – had been sequenced.[180] Diagnostic tests based on the PCR followed soon after, greatly facilitating the control of the spread of the infection. Some 10 months later, at what was termed 'warp speed', vaccines based on revolutionary new technologies were developed. They were demonstrated to be up to 95 per cent effective in preventing severe disease and death.[181]

Within the next few months, vaccine manufacturers were selling billions of doses of vaccine, chiefly to wealthier developed nations.[182] A mathematical modelling study has estimated that about 20 million lives were saved during the first year of the vaccine rollout alone.[183]

Six months into the pandemic many lives were being saved as a result of scientific advances in treating patients, such as the value of steroids in treating the more advanced stages of the disease, followed soon after by antiviral drugs such as Paxlovid and therapeutic monoclonal antibodies. As damaging as the Covid-19 pandemic has been, it is difficult to imagine how humankind would have fared had the SARS-CoV-2 virus afflicted the era of 1918/1919 when it was not even known that Spanish influenza was due to a virus. (Influenza virus was first isolated in 1933.)

Coronaviruses

Before the turn of the century, coronaviruses occupied a relatively minor niche in medical virology. Some four species of coronavirus, well known for some time to be endemic in humans, were responsible for low-priority, relatively mild illnesses – the common cold and mild gastroenteritis. In lecturing to undergraduates, coronaviruses would take up a few minutes of curriculum time.

The first epidemic of coronavirus, in 2003, SARS-CoV-1, caused some international concern because of the high mortality rate of 9.6 per cent. However, the epidemic was soon brought under control after 8 098 cases, predominantly in the Far East. After it disappeared interest in the virus largely waned. Similarly, with the next coronavirus epidemic a decade later, MERS (Middle Eastern Respiratory Syndrome) was also brought under control, albeit with a higher mortality of 34 per cent after 2 492 cases.[184]

Origin of Covid-19: lab-leak theory versus zoonotic spillover theory

Why did SARS-CoV-2 succeed in causing the devastating Covid-19 pandemic, unlike its related predecessors? Two theories for the origin have been put forward – the lab-leak theory and the zoonotic spillover theory. The lab-leak theory postulates that the SARS-CoV-2 virus, or a closely related virus, accidentally escaped from the Wuhan Institute of Virology laboratory in China, where researchers were working with the virus at the time, and seeded itself into the human population. It was to be expected that investigations to further elucidate this theory would be highly sensitive politically. Several visits and inspections by the WHO and other international authorities to the institute were carried out but failed to find evidence to support the accidental leak of a virus.[185]

The second theory, zoonotic spillover, appears to enjoy more solid scientific support.[186] The natural reservoir of a number of pathogenic coronaviruses, including both SARS-CoV-1 and SARS-CoV-2, is the horseshoe bat (genus *Rhinolophus*).[187] The route to humans is probably via an intermediate host. In the case of SARS-CoV-1, the intermediate host was established to be the civet cat, which is sold widely for consumption in the wet markets of the Far East. To date, an intermediate host for SARS-CoV-2 has not yet been established.[188]

The question as to whether these investigations into the origin of the Covid-19 pandemic are merely an exercise of academic interest, or even only to satisfy curiosity, has been raised, as well as whether scientific energies and research funds should rather be focused on improving the current management of the outbreak. There may be an argument in these questions but, in fact, understanding precisely the factors that lead up to pandemics such as Covid-19 is important for developing the necessary preparations for future pandemic threats.[189]

Is the Covid-19 pandemic fizzling itself out?

Clearly, the Covid-19 pandemic was greatly reduced in its toll of human illness and death as it entered into its third year in 2023. Does this suggest that SARS-CoV-2 is evolving towards a more benign endemic coronavirus to join its four other endemic coronavirus compatriots?[190] There certainly is a great deal of evidence to support this optimistic expectation.[191] For example, animal models have demonstrated that the latest variants and sub-units intrinsically cause less severe disease and display a lesser tendency to infect lower respiratory tissue such as the lung – a marker of a more severe outcome.[192]

In addition, the prevalence of antibodies in the population globally is very high and to a great extent reduced the severity of the 2023 outbreak. A study of a South African blood donor population found antibodies to SARS-CoV-2 in 98 per cent of specimens,[193] and a similar study of blood donors in the US found 95 per cent of blood specimens had antibodies.[194]

As yet no new variants of SARS-CoV-2 have appeared after omicron was detected in November 2021, and the evolution of the virus has still only yielded subvariants of the omicron variant, and these have not been associated with more severe disease. However, continuing vigilance and surveillance of the genetic structure of virus isolates is crucial to detect new variants at the earliest possible stage, as there is the possibility that they may not necessarily share the same benign personality as the latest omicron variant.

Covid-19 and the scientific dividends

The Covid-19 pandemic was unprecedented in many respects. What has been most striking to scientific workers in the field has been the unparalleled vast mobilisation of the global biomedical workforce into Covid-19 research. In many institutions around the world, scientists from a variety of fields were reassigned to the Covid-19 bench and the NICD was no exception. The output of scientific research exploded accordingly. In a recent publication it was shown that fully one-fifth of citations in 2020–2021 came from Covid-19-related scientific papers.[195] Even more astonishing was that 98 of the 100 most cited papers throughout all of science over this time were related to Covid-19!

How did the NICD, the flagship public health organisation dealing with communicable diseases, fare during the Covid pandemic? At the outset, it should be mentioned that the institute was a member of a large team tackling the Covid crisis, comprising almost all of the country's medical academic and research centres. An example of this teamwork was the consortium established to carry out genomic analysis of virus isolates derived from clinical specimens and environmental specimens (from wastewater, discussed later in this chapter). The consortium was called the Network for Genomic Surveillance South Africa (NGS-SA) and was made up of participants from the virology departments of the seven medical schools.

The country was fortunate to have highly advanced technological expertise in molecular biology which had been built up from years of HIV/AIDS research. The Covid-19 molecular laboratories at the NICD were led by Professor Penny Moore, who had already made major scientific breakthroughs in HIV research, as mentioned in Chapter 6. The NGS-SA was the first in the world to identify two of the four new SARS-CoV-2 variants – the beta variant and the omicron variant.

Similarly, the Centre for Respiratory Diseases and Meningitis of the NICD has built up advanced expertise over many years of experience investigating and researching bacterial and viral respiratory infections.

Two senior members of that centre, Professor Cheryl Cohen and Professor Anne von Gottberg, published extensively on Covid-19 in South Africa and participated in international fora such as those of the WHO. They were also involved as key advisers to health authorities in South Africa and participated in many media interviews, keeping the public apprised of developments.

The Covid-19 pandemic also saw the establishment of the South African Covid-19 modelling consortium. This was a joint programme comprised of biomathematicians and epidemiologists from the NICD and the universities of Cape Town and Pretoria, which closely monitored and tracked epidemic trends. Modelling exercises were able to provide valuable insights into the growth and the future trajectory of the pandemic as well as the success of interventions such as vaccination and social distancing measures. During the pandemic, the NICD provided weekly epidemiological briefs, including reports on the surveillance of all respiratory pathogens.

The pandemic also reawakened interest in the valuable tool of wastewater surveillance for the detection of pathogens circulating in the community. The sampling of water from sewage treatment plants was pioneered by the global polio eradication campaign, as discussed in chapters 4 and 7.[196] As SARS-CoV-2 is excreted in stool, wastewater sampling proved to be a valuable tool for establishing the extent of circulation of the virus in the population. In addition, it provided viral material enabling genomic sequencing studies to be carried out to monitor for the advent of a new variant or subvariant of the virus.

Over and above the gargantuan mass of scientific productivity, a huge amount has also been learned about the societal aspects of the pandemic. Two very important lessons, in particular, which need to be taken out of experiences of the Covid-19 pandemic are worth highlighting here.

Why are vaccines a free-market commodity?

One thing that should be prevented from happening again in a future pandemic is the tragedy of inequity of resources, as was experienced with Covid vaccine distribution and availability.[197] Tragically, no sooner were Covid-19 vaccines rolled out in early 2021 than wealthy countries plundered the storehouse and greedily hoarded vaccines, in some cases ordering and receiving three to five times what was needed to vaccinate their entire populations. A new term sprang up – 'vaccine nationalism'.[198] The inequity was further aggravated by the corporate greed of the pharmaceutical companies who bullied smaller and less well-heeled countries into having to accept less favourable purchasing conditions for their vaccine supplies.

As a result, low-income countries and, to a significant extent, even middle-income countries were deprived of much-needed vaccine supplies, especially in the critical earlier stages of the pandemic. Later in the pandemic, the situation did improve to some extent as manufacturers acquired the ability to pump out, and of course sell, millions of doses of vaccine. Yet, even as late as 8 July 2022, over 70 per cent of eligible citizens of the US had been fully vaccinated as compared to less than 15 per cent in Africa. COVAX, a programme established by the WHO, GAVI and the Coalition for Epidemic Preparedness Innovations (CEPI), attempted to address this shameful inequity, but with little or only moderate success.

Unfortunately, political expediency trumped scientific common sense, let alone humanity. Global travel has shrunk the planet and greatly increased interactions between the populations of developed and developing countries. The aphorism 'no one is safe until everyone is safe' is especially pertinent for global health. It is precisely those people living in under-resourced and deprived environments, generally accompanied by a higher proportion of immunosuppressed individuals, who are likely to become chronically infected with the virus; and it is chronically infected individuals who are likely to provide sanctuary for SARS-CoV-2 to persist, multiply and potentially generate threatening new variants.

As long as vaccines are treated as marketable commercial commodities, the challenge of vaccine inequity will be difficult to overcome.[199] As long as profits and returns to shareholders trump global public health interests, the inequities of the maldistribution of resources will continue. And one can only but ponder why the first Covid-19 vaccines could be developed in under a year after isolating the virus, but, after close on a further two years, there has been relatively little improvement in the original vaccine. The archaic strain from the Wuhan outbreak is still being used in current vaccines despite the growing ineffectiveness of this vaccine strain to protect against infection with the most recently evolving variants. (Updated vaccine strains have now been incorporated into newer vaccines which are available and in routine use in wealthier developed countries.)

Health communication and societal responsibility

The second important social lesson learned from the Covid-19 pandemic which needs to be addressed in preparing for a future pandemic is the urgent need for improvements in communication. The success or failure of public health measures, over and above the scientific prowess to provide the most effective tools, is directly dependent on the level of support of the population. There can be no doubt that modern communication channels, including social media, have been exploited by anti-science dissidents, including anti-vaxers, who prey on the gaps left by evidence-based medicine communication.

Sadly, throughout the world, there have even been members of the medical profession who have, regrettably, also contributed to mistrust and confusion in the public by almost obsessively taking every opportunity in the public media to berate and undermine the Covid-19 management programmes in their countries.

Particularly unfortunate in South Africa, because of the damage to public trust, were the inappropriate and unfounded acrimonious attacks on the Department of Health and the minister of health's Advisory Committee on Vaccines.[200] The first batch of vaccine to arrive in South Africa consisted of a million doses of the AstraZeneca vaccine, which was earmarked to vaccinate the highest-priority group, the frontline healthcare workers. Unfortunately, laboratory tests indicated that this vaccine was almost totally ineffective against the beta variant of the virus, which was the dominant variant circulating in South Africa at that time.[201] Furthermore, there was no evidence from any human studies that the AstraZeneca vaccine would have any meaningful effectiveness in preventing mild, moderate or severe disease caused by this variant. Consequently, the decision was taken to sell this vaccine to African countries to the north which had struggled to acquire any stocks of vaccine, and where the beta variant had not yet circulated. The reasons behind the decision were explained by myself in a leading article in the *South African Medical Journal* where I made an earnest plea in the public interest to dial down the damaging rhetoric coming from some health professionals.[202]

In reality, there was only a few days' delay before an effective replacement vaccine, the Janssen (Johnson & Johnson) vaccine, became available to vaccinate frontline healthcare workers. Professors Glenda Gray and Linda Gail-Bekker, respectively from the MRC and the University of Cape Town, had fortunately demonstrated in South African trials that the Janssen vaccine was suitably effective against both mild and severe disease due to the beta variant.[203]

It is abundantly clear that an essential part of future pandemic preparedness plans is making provision for professional teams, from the scientific to the sociological, to effectively communicate evidence-based, authentic and non-confusing harm-prevention messages.

EPILOGUE

The fight against the invisible enemy is still very much with us. Many battles have surely been won and countless lives have been saved through scientific progress. Life expectancy globally has gone from 58.6 years a hundred years ago to 79.3 years today. This has been due to a combination of improvements in food supply, provision of clean water, healthier lifestyles and, of course, enormous gains in preventive and curative healthcare, including advances in controlling communicable diseases. However, much still needs to be done, especially in the developing world and in deprived communities.

How far can humankind go in its battle against the unseen enemy of viruses and microbes? The enemy cannot be totally vanquished, and substantial challenges remain. One daunting challenge for contemporary healthcare workers in the third decade of the twenty-first century is the scourge of multi-resistant bacterial infections resulting from overuse or abuse of the antibiotics designed to treat these infections. In battle parlance, the term is 'friendly fire'. After decades of research, effective vaccines against HIV/AIDS and TB still need to be designed, produced and distributed to where the need is greatest. And humankind remains vulnerable to new infectious diseases introduced from animal sources.

However, coming out of the recent Covid-19 pandemic and looking back at our responses to many other epidemics and communicable disease outbreaks, we can take home several valuable lessons. What is now abundantly clear is that the fight against the unseen enemy must be fought on a considerably broader front than only discovering and producing new and effective antimicrobial drugs and vaccines. The war has to be contested on a more holistic battlefront. Winning will only come if all three contributions to the battle are given equal urgency: (1) the scientific contribution, to provide the necessary advanced resources; (2) the general public's contribution, to support implementation; and (3) the politico-economic contribution, for the necessary material resources.

1. THE SCIENTIFIC CONTRIBUTION

The empirical vaccines of the twentieth century demonstrated spectacular success in eradicating smallpox and eliminating several childhood communicable diseases from large swathes of the planet. The simple process of making vaccines by growing organisms and either killing or chemically activating them, or by empirically modifying them by growing them in an unusual environment so that they remain alive and able to multiply but not cause disease, was very effective in the past against many pathogenic organisms. However, this twentieth-century technology is now facing more and more unyielding opponents.

The burgeoning sciences of immunology, genomics and proteomics will further advance the control of communicable diseases going forward in the twenty-first century. New horizons will open up for the future of vaccine development. Empirical vaccine development of the past will give way to precision vaccines of the future, making use of immunology and genomics to identify essential targets that are stable and not subject to the vulnerability of the organism's genetic changes. New routes for administering vaccines other than by injection will be developed for future vaccines. These new procedures for administering vaccines will not only simplify vaccine administration but, importantly, will aim at targeting the mucosal immune system, which is the immune system gateway at the portals of entry into the body, such as the respiratory tract. This could make for more effective vaccines by protecting against infection as well as preventing illness.

Laboratory diagnostic technologies have already moved well away from the classical techniques, and the identification of pathogens has been supplanted by molecular tools such as PCR and on-site rapid diagnostic technologies.

2. THE COMMUNITY CONTRIBUTION

A serious weakness in the battle against communicable diseases, very apparent in recent times, has been the decline of community support and involvement; in all too many cases it has even been a fifth column in the war against microbes. In Chapter 7 we saw how the supportive role of the population contributed so significantly to the success of the smallpox eradication campaign, in contrast to the campaign setbacks in the polio eradication campaign, which came from community obstacles ranging from apathy to violent resistance. It is certainly true that the greater visibility of smallpox substantially aided public support, as compared to the less-conspicuous polio. However, this further emphasises precisely why peer communication, preferably using trusted communicators such as community leaders, plays such a crucial role in these campaigns. The tools of modern communication are, sadly, in so many cases, being used to turn the fight against the invisible enemy into a war on science.

The current Covid-19 pandemic has eminently demonstrated the urgent need to bring together communication professionals and scientists and to combine their skills and knowledge to plan for societal buy-in for the future. The science of communication is a well-developed and well-researched discipline and has demonstrated its effectiveness in the consumer industries. It was largely underutilised in the Covid-19 pandemic, however, and, unfortunately, the science of communication and the psychology of persuasion proved to be highly effective and persuasive in the anti-science lobby.

The science behind infection control measures is often complex and sometimes even perceived by members of the public to be illogical. The purpose of effective science communication is to provide the general public with palatable, evidence-based knowledge with which to make rational choices. Without neglecting the fundamental right of choice in a free society, the making of that choice should be based on authentic, valid and intelligible information, especially when decisions around restrictive behavioural changes need to be made. Both the apathy, due to the lack of information, and the activism, due to misinformation, need to be effectively countered.

3. THE ECONOMIC COMPONENT

The place of market economics as a partner in the control of communicable diseases has benefits and drawbacks. By definition, the system of market economics is founded on the forces of supply and demand to produce the goods and services dictated by the market. In responding to the challenges of the Covid-19 pandemic, one can well see the value of the commercial enterprise, which produced effective vaccines at an unprecedented speed of less than 10 months. Not to be outdone, commercial diagnostic manufacturers were similarly able to produce diagnostic kits within a few months after the isolation of the virus, enabling widespread diagnostic testing in laboratories throughout the world and epidemiological control.

The effectiveness of market forces in providing these products is indisputable, and producing the necessary tools rapidly and effectively is a powerful accessory to the response to communicable diseases.

There is, however, another side, a negative side, to the contribution of market economics to the management of communicable diseases. This is the demonstrated deficiency of the moral ideal of equity. As discussed in Chapter 8, the gross inequity of Covid-19 vaccine distribution, which led to vaccine nationalism and vaccine hoarding by wealthy countries, is a serious concern for global health.

Perhaps now is the time for wise heads to be put together to examine whether there are alternatives to the present system of managing vaccines as commercial commodities and subjecting their development and distribution to market forces. Of course, this applies equally to other health-related materials, which are also subject to the same market forces. Equity when it comes to communicable diseases, however, is more than just a moral imperative; it is also a pragmatic requirement for effective control to provide benefits equally to all humankind.

'We are only safe when everyone is safe' is no more pertinent than when applied to communicable diseases. Internationally, a mindset needs to be created of global pragmatic altruism.

THE NICD AND SOCIETY

What space does the NICD occupy in the public health system of society? By definition, the NICD is a public health institution and it was one of the earliest members, and indeed also a board member, of the IANPHI.

However, being limited to communicable diseases, the NICD's scope of activities is not as broad as many public health institutions abroad. Essentially, the institute is a hybrid of a laboratory-based scientific centre of excellence combined with a public health outreach. Its roles and responsibilities can be compartmentalised into five components:

Public health

The public health responsibility of the NICD rests on the prevention of outbreaks of infectious diseases through surveillance for early warning signals, as well as charting the spread of infections and monitoring the effectiveness of control measures.

Specialised laboratory support

The NICD serves as a referral facility for the clinical/curative and preventive/public health systems of the country and the region. It provides laboratory support for special investigations of biological materials – infectious agents and human and environmental materials. Many of its laboratories serve as regional reference laboratories for the WHO (see Appendix 2).

Training

Together with the academic centres of the medical schools of the country, as well as the universities of technology, undergraduate and postgraduate training is provided to medical and allied professions, as well as epidemiological training for field epidemiologists (as mentioned in Chapter 4).

Research

As a centre of excellence, the NICD has contributed extensively to the South African research output on communicable diseases, especially those of relevance to this part of the world.

Communication

The outreach to the general public is the most visible responsibility of the NICD to society and is, at the same time, its most challenging.

THE COVID-19 INFODEMIC AND ANTI-SCIENCE

The word 'infodemic' was born in 2003 and has come to describe the twenty-first-century phenomenon of the virtually instantaneous electronic transmission of information via the internet and social media. The WHO regarded the infodemic as a major global health threat and in February 2020 defined the term as follows:

> ... too much information including false or misleading information in digital and physical environments during a disease outbreak. It causes confusion and risk-taking behaviour that can harm health. It also leads to mistrust in health authorities and undermines the public health response.[204]

The Covid-19 pandemic, more than any previous health issue, strikingly highlighted the critical public health importance of supplying credible, scientific and evidence-based information that is, at the same time, palatable, understandable and effective. Prior to Covid-19, the damage resulting from vaccine hesitancy was clearly shown through routine childhood immunisation programmes. A study in the US demonstrated that even small declines in vaccination coverage in children due to vaccine hesitancy could have substantial public health and economic consequences.[205]

The fallout from Covid-19 vaccine hesitancy in adults has been even larger. Internationally, and in South Africa, muscular organisations and aggressive individuals campaigned relentlessly against the life-saving Covid-19 vaccination campaigns. Vaccine coverage fell well short of planned targets in South Africa and globally and, tragically, millions of doses of vaccine had to be discarded as a result. How much of the vaccination shortfall was contributed to by apathy and how much by anti-vaccination sentiment varied among different communities.

There can be no doubt that misinformation and false claims played a significant role. Conspiracy theories abounded about the nefarious motives of the pharmaceutical industry. The speed at which Covid-19 vaccines were produced gave rise to wild rumours about the danger of these new vaccines, including the allegation that the nucleic-acid-based vaccines, the mRNA vaccines, produced by Pfizer and Moderna, would remain permanently in the body, integrate into the genetic material of the vaccine recipient and ultimately cause long-lasting damage.

Once these rumours were embedded in the public mind, scientific information – for example, showing that the mRNA of the vaccine was rapidly eliminated from the body – often failed to correct damaging false information. Campaigns citing human rights and personal choice were vigorously exploited. The ethical tensions between vaccination decisions and policies versus individual rights and community obligations for harm prevention were recognised early in the pandemic.[206]

Medical quackery in the twenty-first century

The pernicious effects of hostility to science and the fallout from misinformation and mistrust during the Covid-19 pandemic era caused similar damage when it popularised ineffective and potentially toxic medicines. In the early stages of the pandemic, the anti-malarial/anti-rheumatic drugs chloroquine and hydroxychloroquine were shown to inhibit coronavirus in the laboratory. However, despite having demonstrated complete ineffectiveness in several clinical trials and in some causing severe toxicity to the heart and the retina, the agent was still widely touted for the prevention and treatment of Covid-19. The issue also became highly politicised, with the presidents of the US and France lending their support for these drugs.[207]

No sooner had interest waned in chloroquine than it was replaced by an even more extensively misused and touted cure. This was the drug ivermectin, which is used mainly by veterinarians to treat worm infestations in animals. It is only rarely used in humans for the treatment of some tropical worm infestations. Many control trials in a variety of subjects and settings showed no effectiveness whatsoever in preventing or treating SARS-CoV-2 infection.[208] As was the case with chloroquine, ivermectin was not entirely harmless and occasionally was accompanied by moderate to severe toxicity.[209]

The challenge of providing effective health science communication to the public is certainly formidable. The anti-science/mistrust lobby is a powerful one and even became threatening to Covid experts. In the Preface, I mentioned that the well-known infectious diseases expert Dr Anthony Fauci had to be provided with a security detail because of death threats to him and his family. In a recent study of over 300 scientists in the US, two of three reported harassment of one sort or another from the public, and 15 per cent reported death threats.[210]

The NICD with its limited resources contributes valiantly to the fight against misinformation. Members of staff are regularly interviewed in electronic and print media and the institute website (www.nicd.ac.za) is replete with informative material and up-to-date data. Similar efforts are also made by academic and research institutions throughout the country, as well as governmental bodies, including the Department of Health.

However, communication from centres of excellence and authorities enjoys limited success in meaningfully educating the broader public.

During the Covid pandemic, efforts were made to disseminate information through trusted messengers such as teachers and community leaders. Unfortunately, this was clearly insufficient to counter the persistent anti-science lobby. Innovative communication planning is urgently needed before the next pandemic.

THE NICD: PREPAREDNESS FOR THE NEXT PANDEMIC

Pandemics of new infectious diseases feature prominently among the biggest threats to the future survival of the human race in the lists of the 10 most serious threats to humanity published by think-tanks such as the Davos agenda of the World Economic Forum,[211] the Centre for the Study of Existential Risk,[212] the Commission for the Human Future,[213] and the Global Challenges Foundation.[214]

The recent Covid-19 pandemic graphically demonstrated the devastation in costs of lives lost and costs to economies as a result of being largely unprepared for a new infectious disease, even in a scientifically advanced modern world. Close to seven million deaths from Covid-19 were recorded as of 30 July 2023;[215] there is no doubt that the true death toll is an order of magnitude higher than that number. The economic fallout has similarly been alarming. The International Monetary Fund projected the economic global decline to be the worst since the Great Depression of the 1930s.[216] South Africa's GDP by the end of 2020 was estimated to have declined by five per cent due to Covid-19.[217]

At the height of the Covid-19 pandemic in March 2021, 25 heads of government, including the president of South Africa, signed an appeal calling for the international community to establish a treaty that would create structures for pandemic preparedness and response. The aim of this international treaty, which is still in the making, would be to promote a comprehensive and multi-sectoral global health structure to strengthen national, regional and global capacities to effectively respond to future pandemics. All the ingredients for another pandemic in the not-too-distant future – population overcrowding in much of the world, increasing exposure to exotic animals, climate change and international travel – are already in place. Those who control the purse strings of public spending therefore need to look very carefully at the cost to the country of pandemic communicable diseases.

The erstwhile Covid-19 pandemic has demonstrated the critical role of an institution such as the NICD for the health of the country, in addition to its value regionally and globally. Unfortunately, the institute wrestles with the same financial straitjacket common to all public entities.

While committees formed in many countries to prepare for a forthcoming pandemic are important, at the end of the day it is public health institutions like the NICD that will play the critical role in sounding the alert of a forthcoming pandemic and then play a crucial role in its management.

In addition, as was illustrated in chapters 2 and 3, it is vital that public health institutions are not weighed down by bureaucratic constraints which prevent them from reaching their full potential. As this narrative has shown over and over again, independence and autonomy are critical if the NICD is to give of its best for the country and for global health. Hindsight is 20/20 and the value of examining history is in order to improve the future. The barrier of trust will need to be overcome for the benefit of all. This is pertinent to the future of the NICD and its notable contribution to the health of the nation.

NATIONAL INSTITUTE FOR COMMUNICABLE DISEASES

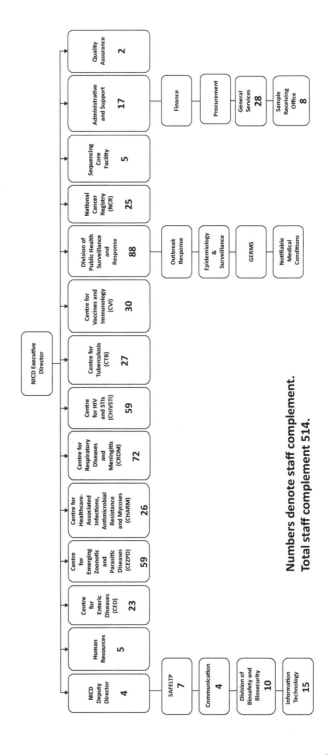

Numbers denote staff complement.
Total staff complement 514.

WORLD HEALTH ORGANIZATION REFERENCE LABORATORIES SITED IN THE NICD

NICD Centre	WHO Reference Laboratory
Centre for Tuberculosis (TB)	WHO TB Supranational Reference Laboratory Network (SRLN)
Centre for Vaccines and Immunology (CVI)	WHO Polio Reference Laboratory
Centre for Vaccines and Immunology (CVI)	WHO Measles Regional Reference Laboratory
Centre for Respiratory Diseases (CRDM)	WHO/National Influenza Centre
Centre for Respiratory Diseases (CRDM)	WHO/AFRO Reference Laboratory – RSV
Centre for Respiratory Diseases (CRDM)	WHO/AFRO Reference Laboratory – SARS-CoV-2
Centre for Respiratory Diseases (CRDM)	WHO Vaccine-Preventable Invasive Bacterial Diseases (VP-IBD) Regional Reference Laboratory
Centre for Emerging Zoonotic and Parasitic Diseases (CEZPD) – Arboviruses	WHO Reference Laboratory – awaiting renewal
Centre for Emerging Zoonotic and Parasitic Diseases (CEZPD) – Special Bacterial	WHO Plague Reference Laboratory
Centre for Healthcare-Associated Infections, Antimicrobial Resistance and Mycoses	WHO Antimicrobial Resistance (AMR) Surveillance and Quality Assessment Collaborating Centres Network
Centre for HIV and STIs (CHIVSTI) – HIV drug resistance	WHO Reference Laboratory

NOTES

PREFACE

1   CDC. 'David J. Sencer CDC Museum: Our History – Our Story'. 19 April 2023, https://www.cdc.gov/museum/history/our-story.html, accessed 22 May 2023.

2   Marais Malan, *In Quest of Health: The South African Institute for Medical Research 1912–1973* (Johannesburg: Lowry Publishers, 1988).

3   Salim S. Abdool Karim and Tulio de Oliveira, 'New SARS-COV-2 Variants – Clinical, Public Health, and Vaccine Implications', *New England Journal of Medicine* 384, no. 19 (2021): 1866–1868, https://doi.org/10.1056/nejmc2100362.

4   Marcia McNutt and Michael M. Crow, 'Enhancing Trust in Science and Democracy in an Age of Misinformation', *Issues in Science and Technology* 29, no. 3 (2023): 18–20, https://doi.org/10.58875/fabl6884.

5   Chaomei Chen, *Mapping Scientific Frontiers: The Quest for Knowledge Visualization* (London: Springer, 2017), 135.

6   Jack Metz and Barry D. Schoub, 'James Gear – An Appreciation', *South African Medical Journal* 70, no. 4 (1986): 6–7.

7   Barry D. Schoub, 'Professor HJ Koornhof – A Tribute and an Appreciation', *South African Medical Journal* 97, no. 11 (2007): 1113.

INTRODUCTION

8   Barry D. Schoub, *Medical Virology: The Coming of Age: Inaugural Lecture* (Johannesburg: Witwatersrand University Press, 1983).

9   Wikipedia, 'Lord Kelvin', 2023, https://en.wikipedia.org/wiki/Lord_Kelvin, accessed 20 August 2023.

10 Wikiquote, 'Albert A. Michelson', 2023, https://en.wikiquote.org/wiki/Albert_A._Michelson, accessed 20 August 2023.

11 Mitchell L. Cohen, 'Changing Patterns of Infectious Disease', *Nature* 406, no. 6797 (2000): 762, https://doi.org/10.1038/35021206.

12 Brad Spellberg, 'Dr. William H. Stewart: Mistaken or Maligned?' *Clinical Infectious Diseases* 47, no. 2 (2008): 294, https://doi.org/10.1086/589579.

13 David I. Watkins, 'The Vaccine Search Goes On', *Scientific American* 299, no. 5 (2008): 69, https://doi.org/10.1038/scientificamerican1108-69.

14   Saloni Ritchie et al., 'Causes of Death', *Our World in Data*, 2018, https://ourworld indata.org/causes-of-death, accessed 22 May 2023.

15   Catherine M. Michaud, 'Global Burden of Infectious Diseases', in *Encyclopedia of Microbiology* 3rd ed., ed. Moselio Schaechter (Amsterdam: Academic Press, 2009), 444–454, https://doi.org/10.1016/b978-012373944-5.00185-1.

16   IANPHI, *Progress Report 2022*, 2022, https://www.ianphi.org/, accessed 22 May 2023.

17   CDC, 'David J. Sencer CDC Museum: Our History – Our Story', 19 April 2023, https://www.cdc.gov/museum/history/our-story.html, accessed 22 May 2023.

18   McNutt and Crow, 'Enhancing Trust'.

19   Sarah Boon, '21st Century Science Overload'. Canadian Science Publishing (blog), 7 January 2018, http://blog.cdnsciencepub.com/21st-century-science-overload/, accessed 22 May 2023.

20   John P.A. Ioannidis et al., 'Massive Covidization of Research Citations and the Citation Elite', *Proceedings of the National Academy of Sciences* 119, no. 28 (2022): e2204074119, https://doi.org/10.1073/pnas.2204074119.

21   Courtney Temple, Ruby Hoang and Robert G. Hendrickson, 'Toxic Effects from Ivermectin Use Associated with Prevention and Treatment of COVID-19', *New England Journal of Medicine* 385, no. 23 (2021), 2197–2198, https://doi.org/10.1056/nejmc2114907.

22   Robert M. Wachter, 'Nailing the Nuance on COVID-19', *Science* 337 (2022): 243.

23   Jeffrey D. Sachs et al., 'The Lancet Commission on Lessons for the Future from the COVID-19 Pandemic', *The Lancet* 400, no. 10359 (2022): 1224–1280, https://doi.org/10.1016/50140-6736(22)01585-9.

CHAPTER 1 The early seeds

24   Malan, *In Quest of Health*.

25   Jack Metz, *South Africa's Health Sentinel: The South African Institute for Medical Research 1974 to 1999* (Johannesburg: Adler Museum of Medicine, 2017).

26   Howard Phillips, *Plague, Pox and Pandemics: A Jacana Pocket History of Epidemics in South Africa* (Auckland Park: Jacana, 2012).

27   Aaron E. Klein, *Trial by Fury: The Polio Vaccine Controversy* (New York: Scribner, 1972), 4.

28   James H.S. Gear, *The History of the Poliomyelitis Research Foundation* (Johannesburg: The Poliomyelitis Research Foundation, 1996), https://doi.org/10.1093/cid/civ568.

29   Gear, *The History of the Poliomyelitis Research Foundation*.

30   Leonard L. Alexander, 'East London Complaint: Further Statement by the Minister', *South African Medical Journal* 29, no. 36 (1955): 848–849.

31   Gear, *The History of the Poliomyelitis Research Foundation*.

32   For details of the research-supporting activities and the various research and training grants offered by the PRF, refer to the website https://www.prf.ac.za.

CHAPTER 2 The National Institute for Virology

33   James S. Gear et al., 'Outbreak of Marburg Virus Disease in Johannesburg', *BMJ* 4, no. 5995 (1975): 489–493, https://doi.org/:10.1136/bmj.4.5995.489.

34   International Commission, 'Ebola Haemorrhagic Fever in Zaire, 1976', *Bulletin of the World Health Organization* 56, no. 2 (1978): 271–293.

35   Chandré Gould et al., *Project Coast: Apartheid's Chemical and Biological Warfare Programme* (Geneva: United Nations Publications, 2002).

36   Letter from the Department of Health to Barry Schoub, 5 November 1991 (translated from Afrikaans).

37   Government correspondence, Permission for Participation in Radio Programme, Department of Health to NIV Director, 13 March 1991.

38   Government correspondence, Permission for Participation in Radio Programme, Dr P.G. Jupp to NIV Director, 15 January 1990.

39   Government correspondence, Rationalisation and Position of the NIV, NIV Director to the Department of Health, 2 March 1990.

40   Personal correspondence, Steyn.let/91, 10 December 1991.

41   Personal correspondence, Response to invitation, Peter Piot to Barry Schoub, 23 November 1987.

42   Personal correspondence, Response to invitation, Geoffrey Rose to Barry Schoub, 17 December 1987.

CHAPTER 3 Putting together the National Institute for Communicable Diseases

43   African National Congress, *A National Health Plan for South Africa* (Johannesburg: African National Congress, 1994).

44   African National Congress, *A National Health Plan*, 43.

45   IANPHI, *Building Global Public Health Capacity,* 2023, https://www.ianphi.org/, accessed 22 May 2023.

46   Peter Bloland et al., 'The Role of Public Health Institutions in Global Health System Strengthening Efforts: The US CDC's Perspective', *PLoS Medicine* 9, no. 4 (2012): 1–5, https://doi.org/10.1371/journal.pmed.1001199.

47   Michaud, 'Global Burden of Infectious Diseases'.

48   Hoosen Coovadia et al., 'The Health and Health System of South Africa: Historical Roots of Current Public Health Challenges', *The Lancet* 374, no. 9692 (2009): 817–834, https://doi.org/10.1016/s0140-6736(09)60951-x.

49   Personal correspondence, Letter to the The National Institute for Communicable Diseases, 6 August 1999.

CHAPTER 4 Surveillance of communicable diseases

50   Alexander D. Langmuir, 'The Surveillance of Communicable Diseases of National Importance', *New England Journal of Medicine* 268, no. 4 (1963): 182–183, https://doi.org/10.1056/nejm196301242680405.

51   Oliver W. Morgan et al., 'How Better Pandemic and Epidemic Intelligence Will Prepare the World for Future Threats', *Nature Medicine* 28, no. 8 (2022): 1526–1528, https://doi.org/10.1038/s41591-022-01900-5.

52   Joshua I. Levy et al., 'Wastewater Surveillance for Public Health', *Science* 379, no. 6627 (2023): 26–27, https://doi.org/10.1126/science.ade2503.

53 Amanda L. Wilkinson et al., 'Surveillance to Track Progress Toward Polio Eradication–Worldwide, 2020–2021', *Morbidity and Mortality Weekly Report* 71, no. 15 (2022): 538–544, https://doi.org/10.15585/mmwr.mm7115a2.

54 Johanna M. McAnerney, Sylvia Johnson and Barry D. Schoub, 'Surveillance of Respiratory Viruses: A 10-Year Laboratory-Based Study', *South African Medical Journal* 84, no. 8 Pt 1 (1994): 473–477; Eric Budgell et al., 'Evaluation of Two Influenza Surveillance Systems in South Africa', *PLoS One* 10, no. 3 (2015): e0120226, https://doi.org/10.1371/journal.pone.0120226.

55 WHO, 'Recommended Composition of Influenza Virus Vaccines for Use in the 2023 Southern Hemisphere Influenza Season', 23 September 2022, accessed 15 January 2024, https://cdn.who.int/media/docs/default-source/influenza/who-influenza-re commendations/vcm-southern-hemisphere-recommendation-2023/202209_re commendation.pdf?sfvrsn=83a26d50_3&download=true.

56 Juno Thomas et al., 'Outbreak of Listeriosis in South Africa Associated with Processed Meat', *New England Journal of Medicine* 382, no. 7 (2020): 632–643, https://doi.org/10.1056/nejmoa1907462.

57 Joe Whitworth, 'Court Overturns Decision in Tiger Brands Listeria Case', *Food Safety News,* 7 February 2022, https://www.foodsafetynews.com/2022/02/court-overturns-decision-in-tiger-brands-listeria-case/, accessed 23 May 2023.

58 Jim O'Neill, 'Tackling Drug-Resistant Infections Globally: Final Report and Recommendations', *The Review of Antimicrobial Resistance,* May 2016, https://amr-review.org/sites/default/files/160525Final%20paperwith%20cover.pdf, accessed 23 May 2023.

59 'Prime Minister Warns of Global Threat of Antibiotic Resistance', Press release, 2 July 2014, https://www.gov.uk/government/news/prime-minister-warns-of-global-threat-of-antibiotic-resistance, accessed 23 May 2023.

60 Laura J.V. Piddock, 'The Crisis of No New Antibiotics – What Is the Way Forward?' *The Lancet Infectious Diseases* 12, no. 3 (2012): 249–253, https://doi.org/10.1016/s1473-3099(11)70316-4.

61 Françoise van Bambeke et al., 'Multidrug-Resistant *Streptococcus pneumoniae* Infections: Current and Future Therapeutic Options', *Drugs* 67, no. 16 (2007): 2355–2382, https://doi.org/10.2165/00003495-200767160-00005.

62 Magnus Unemo and Robert A. Nicholas, 'Emergence of Multidrug-Resistant, Extensively Drug-Resistant and Untreatable Gonorrhea', *Future Microbiology* 7, no. 12 (2012): 1401–1422, https://doi.org/10.2217/fmb.12.117.

63 Helen Ayles, Linda Mureithi and Musonda Simwinga, 'The State of Tuberculosis in South Africa: What Does the First National Tuberculosis Prevalence Survey Teach Us?' *The Lancet Infectious Diseases* 22, no. 8 (2022): 1094–1096, https://doi.org/10.1016/s1473-3099(22)00286-9.

64 WHO, *Global Tuberculosis Report.*

65 NICD, 'TB Surveillance Dashboard and Other Resources', 2019, https://www.nicd.ac.za/tb-surveillance-dashboard/, accessed 23 May 2023.

66 Kwonjune J. Seung, Salmaan Keshavjee and Michael L. Rich, 'Multidrug-Resistant Tuberculosis and Extensively Drug-Resistant Tuberculosis', *Cold Spring Harbor Perspectives in Medicine* 5, no. 9 (2015), https://doi.org/10.1101/cshperspect.a017863.

67 UNAIDS, *South Africa 2021,* 2021, https://www.unaids.org/en/regionscountries/countries/southafrica, accessed 23 May 2023.

68 'Viral suppression' means that, as a result of antiretroviral treatment, the amount of virus in the body is drastically reduced to only a very minimal remnant, allowing the body's immune system to function reasonably well and thus preventing illness. This is generally quantified at demonstrating less than 200 copies of the virus per millilitre of blood.

69 L. Simbayi et al., *South African National HIV Prevalence, Incidence, Behaviour and Communication Survey, 2017: Towards Achieving the UNAIDS 90-90-90 Targets* (Cape Town: HSRC Press, 2019).

70 NICD, *The 2019 National Antenatal HIV Sentinel Survey (ANCHSS) Key Findings*, 30 April 2021, https://www.nicd.ac.za/wp-content/uploads/2021/11/Antenatal-survey-2019-reportFINAL27April21.pdf1, accessed 24 May 2023.

71 WHO, *HIV Drug Resistance: Brief Report 2024*, accessed 26 April 2024, https://www.who.int/publications/i/item/9789240086319.

72 Sheri A. Lippman et al., 'Improvements in the South African HIV Care Cascade: Findings on 90-90-90 Targets from Successive Population-Representative Surveys in North West Province', *Journal of the International AIDS Society* 22, no. 6 (2019), https://doi.org/10.1002/jia2.25295.

73 Gillian M. Hunt et al., 'Provincial and National Prevalence Estimates of Transmitted HIV-1 Drug Resistance in South Africa Measured Using Two WHO-Recommended Methods', *Antiviral Therapy* 24, no. 3 (2018): 203–210, https://doi.org/10.3851/imp3294.

74 Herbert A. Mbunkah et al., 'Low-Abundance Drug-Resistant HIV-1 Variants in Antiretroviral Drug-Naive Individuals: A Systematic Review of Detection Methods, Prevalence, and Clinical Impact', *The Journal of Infectious Diseases* 221, no. 10 (2019): 1584–1597, https://doi.org/10.1093/infdis/jiz650; Selamawit A. Woldesenbet et al., 'Viral Suppression and Factors Associated with Failure to Achieve Viral Suppression among Pregnant Women in South Africa', *AIDS* 34, no. 4 (2020): 589–597, https://doi.org/10.1097/qad.0000000000002457.

75 Paul M. Sharp and Beatrice H. Hahn, 'The Evolution of HIV-1 and the Origin of AIDS', *Philosophical Transactions of the Royal Society B: Biological Sciences* 365, no. 1552 (2010): 2487–2494, https://doi.org/10.1098/rstb.2010.0031.

76 Spyros Lytras et al., 'The Animal Origin of SARS-COV-2', *Science* 373, no. 6558 (2021): 968–970, https://doi.org/10.1126/science.abh0117.

77 John S. Mackenzie and Martyn Jeggo, 'The One Health Approach – Why Is It So Important?' *Tropical Medicine and Infectious Disease* 4, no. 2 (2019): 88–91, https://doi.org/10.3390/tropicalmed4020088.

78 Janusz T. Paweska et al., 'South African Ebola Diagnostic Response in Sierra Leone: A Modular High Biosafety Field Laboratory', *PLOS Neglected Tropical Diseases* 11, no. 6 (2017): e0005665, https://doi.org/10.1371/journal.pntd.0005665.

79 WHO, *World Malaria Report*, 6 December 2021, accessed 1 March 2024, https://www.who.int/teams/global-malaria-programme/reports/world-malaria-report-2021.

80 Ryleen Balawanth et al., 'Assessing Kwa-Zulu-Natal's Progress Towards Malaria Elimination and Its Readiness for Sub-national Verification', *Malaria Journal* 18, no. 1 (2019): 108, https://doi.org/10.1186/s12936-019-2739-5.

81 The poem *The Odyssey*, attributed to Homer, describes the mythical 10 years of travel of the hero Odysseus, as he attempts to return home after the Trojan War.

82   Ashley Burke et al., 'Anopheles parensis Contributes to Residual Malaria Transmission in South Africa', *Malaria Journal* 18, no. 1 (2019): 257, https://doi.org/10.1186/s12936-019-2889-5.

83   Shüné V. Oliver and Basil D. Brooke, 'The Effect of Elevated Temperatures on the Life History and Insecticide Resistance Phenotype of the Major Malaria Vector *Anopheles arabiensis* (Diptera: Culicidae)', *Malaria Journal* 16, no. 1 (2017), https://doi.org/10.1186/s12936-017-1720-4.

84   Leonard C. Dandalo et al., 'Effect of Ionising (Gamma) Radiation on Female *Anopheles arabiensis*', *Transactions of the Royal Society of Tropical Medicine and Hygiene* 111, no. 1 (2017): 38–40, https://doi.org/10.1093/trstmh/trx013.

85   Thabo Mashatola et al., 'A Review on the Progress of Sex-Separation Techniques for Sterile Insect Technique Applications against *Anopheles arabiensis*', *Parasites & Vectors* 11, no. S2 (2018), https://doi.org/10.1186/s13071-018-3219-4.

86   Carl Reddy et al., 'South Africa Field Epidemiology Training Program: Developing and Building Applied Epidemiology Capacity, 2007–2016', *BMC Public Health* 19, no. S3 (2019), https://doi.org/10.1186/s12889-019-6788-z.

CHAPTER 5 The viral haemorrhagic fevers of Africa

87   The virus was named after the town of Marburg in Germany, where the first recognised cases of the disease were diagnosed in 1967. In that outbreak, some 31 laboratory workers, medical personnel and family members in Marburg and Frankfurt in Germany and Belgrade in Yugoslavia (now Serbia), were infected, seven of whom died. The laboratory personnel involved in the outbreak had been handling African green monkeys imported from Uganda.

88   Biological laboratories working with potentially communicable material are classified into four categories, referred to as biosafety levels (BSLs). A BSL-1 laboratory would handle material containing low-risk pathogenic organisms such as the bacterium *E coli*. Standard precautions such as personal protective equipment for laboratory workers, no food or drink in the laboratory would, decontamination of surfaces and so on would be required at this level. A BSL-2 laboratory would, in addition, require work to be performed within a biological safety cabinet with filtered laminar flow air. The majority of clinical specimens would be suitable for work in a BSL-2 laboratory. BSL-3 laboratories are specialised units used for working with high-risk organisms, such as tuberculosis, yellow fever, West Nile virus and so on. A higher grade of personal protective equipment would be required, and significant laboratory modifications would need to be engineered – for example, to create a negative flow environment to direct airflow into the laboratory. The BSL-4 laboratory is the most specialised maximum containment laboratory used for working with the most dangerous of organisms such as the viral haemorrhagic fever viruses.

89   James H. Gear, 'Clinical Aspects of African Viral Hemorrhagic Fevers', *Clinical Infectious Diseases* 11, suppl. 4 (1989), https://doi.org/10.1093/clinids/11.supplement4.s777.

90   Robert Swanepoel et al., 'Investigations Following Initial Recognition of Crimean-Congo Haemorrhagic Fever in South Africa and the Diagnosis of 2 Further Cases', *South African Medical Journal* 68, no. 9 (1985): 638–641.

91 Jean-Jacques Muyembe-Tamfum et al., 'Ebola Outbreak in Kikwit, Democratic Republic of the Congo: Discovery and Control Measures', *The Journal of Infectious Diseases* 179, suppl. 1 (1999): S259–S262, https://doi.org/10.1086/514302.

92 Robert Colebunders et al., 'Marburg Hemorrhagic Fever in Durba and Watsa, Democratic Republic of the Congo: Clinical Documentation, Features of Illness, and Treatment'. *The Journal of Infectious Diseases* 196, suppl. 2 (2007): S148–S153, https://doi.org/10.1086/520543.

93 CDC, 'Marburg Virus Disease Outbreaks', 9 June 2023, https://www.cdc.gov/vhf/marburg/outbreaks/chronology.html, accessed 24 May 2023.

94 Patricia M. Dietz et al., 'Epidemiology and Risk Factors for Ebola Virus Disease in Sierra Leone – 23 May 2014 to 31 January 2015', *Clinical Infectious Diseases* 61, no. 11 (2015): 1648–1654.

95 Paweska et al., 'South African Ebola Diagnostic Response'.

96 Nivesh H. Sewlall and Janusz T. Paweska, 'Lujo Virus: Current Concepts', *Virus Adaptation and Treatment* 9 (2017): 41–47, https://doi.org/10.2147/vaat.s113593.

CHAPTER 6 Facing the HIV/AIDS pandemic

97 Joint United Nations Programme on HIV/AIDS, *UNAIDS Data 2022*, 2022, https://www.unaids.org/sites/default/files/mediaasset/data-book-2022en.pdf, accessed 28 May 2023.

98 UNAIDS, 'Global HIV and AIDS Statistics – Fact Sheet', 2021, https://www.unaids.org/en/resources/fact-sheet, accessed 28 May 2023.

99 CDC, '*Pneumocystis* Pneumonia – Los Angeles', *Morbidity and Mortality Weekly Report* 30, no. 21 (1981): 250–252.

100 CDC, 'Kaposi's Sarcoma and *Pneumocystis* Pneumonia among Homosexual Men – New York City and California', *Morbidity and Mortality Weekly Report* 30, no. 25 (1981): 305–308.

101 Françoise Barré-Sinoussi et al., 'Isolation of a T-lymphotropic Retrovirus from a Patient at Risk for Acquired Immune Deficiency Syndrome (AIDS)', *Science* 220, no. 4599 (1983): 868–871, https://doi.org/10.1126/science.6189183.

102 Gallo's team had been working for some time on the family of human retroviruses (viruses utiising the enzyme reverse transcriptase and associated with tumour formation). HTLV-3 or HIV was the third member of the family identified by the team.

103 Samuel Broder and Robert C. Gallo, 'A Pathogenic Retrovirus (HTLV-III) Linked to AIDS', *New England Journal of Medicine* 311, no. 20 (1984): 1292–1297, https://doi.org/10.1056/nejm198411153112006.

104 François Clavel et al., 'Isolation of a New Human Retrovirus from West African Patients with AIDS', *Science* 233, no. 4761 (1986): 343–346, https://doi.org/10.1126/science.2425430.

105 Sero-archaeological studies examine stored specimens, especially serum samples, for evidence of infection in the past.

106 Tuofu Zhu et al., 'An African HIV-1 Sequence from 1959 and Implications for the Origin of the Epidemic', *Nature* 391, no. 6667 (1998): 594–597, https://doi.org/10.1038/35400.

107 Paul M. Sharp and Beatrice H. Hahn, 'The Evolution of HIV-1 and the Origin of AIDS', *Philosophical Transactions of the Royal Society B: Biological Sciences* 365, no. 1552 (2010): 2487–2494, https://doi.org/10.1098/rstb.2010.0031.

108 A zoonosis is a disease transmitted from animals to humans.

109 Sharp and Hahn, 'The Evolution of HIV-1', 2487–2494.

110 Gerhardus Johannes Ras et al., 'Acquired Immunodeficiency Syndrome: A Report of 2 South African Cases', *South African Medical Journal* 64 (1983): 140–142.

111 Rukhsana Sher et al., 'Lack of Evidence of HIV Infection in Drug Abusers at Present', *South African Medical Journal* 70 (1986): 776–777.

112 Barry D. Schoub et al., 'Absence of HIV Infection in Prostitutes and Women Attending Sexually-Transmitted Disease Clinics in South Africa', *Transactions of the Royal Society of Tropical Medicine and Hygiene* 81, no. 5 (1987): 874–875, https://doi.org/10.1016/0035-9203(87)90057-5.

113 Barry D. Schoub, 'Estimation of the Total Size of the Human Immunodeficiency Virus and Hepatitis B Epidemics in South Africa', *South African Medical Journal* 81 (1991): 63–66.

114 Ayesha B.M. Kharsany et al., 'Community-Based HIV Prevalence in KwaZulu-Natal, South Africa: Results of a Cross-Sectional Household Survey', *The Lancet HIV* 5, no. 8 (2018): e427–e437, https://doi.org/10.1016/s2352-3018(18)30104-8.

115 Human Sciences Research Council, *South African National HIV Prevalence, Incidence, Behaviour and Communication Survey, 2008* (2009), accessed 10 November 2023, https://web.archive.org/web/20100522082857/http:/www.hsrc.ac.za/Document-3238.phtml, accessed 10 November 2023.

116 Frontline, 'Thabo Mbeki's Letter', *Frontline: The Age of AIDS,* 2006, https://www.pbs.org/wgbh/pages/frontline/aids/docs/mbeki.html, accessed 29 May 2023.

117 James Myburgh, 'The Virodene Affair (I)', *Politicsweb,* 17 September 2007, https://www.politicsweb.co.za/news-and-analysis/the-virodene-affair-i, accessed 29 May 2023.

118 Malegapuru W. Makgoba, 'HIV/AIDS: The Peril of Pseudoscience', *Science* 288, no. 5469 (2000): 1171, https://doi.org/10.1126/science.288.5469.1171.

119 'The Durban Declaration', *Nature* 406, no. 6791 (2000): 15–16, https://doi.org/10.1038/35017662.

120 Alastair Thomson, 'Mbeki Address: 13th International AIDS Conference', *Scoop World,* 18 July 2000, https://www.scoop.co.nz/stories/WO0007/S00072/mbeki-address-13th-international-aids-conference.htm, accessed 29 May 2023.

121 *Sunday Independent,* 2 July 2000, 8.

122 Peter Duesberg, born in Germany, was appointed as Professor of Molecular and Cell Biology at the University of California, Berkeley. His earlier career, before AIDS denialism, was distinguished by important advances he made in the molecular biology of cancer. He was elected to the National Academy of Science of the USA and received an Outstanding Researcher Award from the National Institutes of Health. Intellectually he was the most senior member of the AIDS denialists.

123 Charles Geshekter was Professor of History at California State University.

124 AIDS Advisory Panel, *Presidential AIDS Advisory Panel Report,* 2001, https://www.gov.za/sites/default/files/gcisdocument/201409/aidspanelpdf0.pdf, accessed 29 May 2023.

125 Personal correspondence, Dr Harvey Bialy to Barry Schoub, 2001.

126 Personal correspondence, Dr Harvey Bialy to Carolyn Williamson, 2001.

127 Pride Chigwedere et al., 'Estimating the Lost Benefits of Antiretroviral Drug Use in South Africa', *JAIDS Journal of Acquired Immune Deficiency Syndromes* 49, no. 4 (2008): 410–415, https://doi.org/10.1097/qai.0b013e31818a6cd5.

128 Edwin Cameron and Nathan Geffen, *Witness to AIDS* (Grahamstown: South African Library for the Blind, 2006).

129 Stats SA, *Mid-Year Population Estimates 2021*, Statistical Release PO302 2022, http://www.statssa.gov.za/publications/P0302/P03022021.pdf, accessed 29 May 2023.

130 Penny L. Moore et al., 'Evolution of an HIV Glycan-Dependent Broadly Neutralizing Antibody Epitope Through Immune Escape', *Nature Medicine* 18, no. 11 (2012): 1688–1692, https://doi.org/10.1038/nm.2985.

131 NICD, *The 2019 National Antenatal HIV Sentinel Survey*.

132 CDC, 'Moving Towards the UNAIDS 90-90-90 Targets', 14 March 2019, https://www.cdc.gov/globalhealth/stories/2019/moving-towards-unaids.html, accessed 29 May 2023.

133 Gavin George et al., 'Evaluating DREAMS HIV Prevention Interventions Targeting Adolescent Girls and Young Women in High HIV Prevalence Districts in South Africa: Protocol for a Cross-Sectional Study', *BMC Women's Health* 20, no. 1 (2020): 7, https://doi.org/10.1186/s12905-019-0875-2.

134 Hunt et al., 'Provincial and National Prevalence Estimates'.

135 Linda-Gail Bekker et al., 'The Complex Challenges of HIV Vaccine Development Require Renewed and Expanded Global Commitment', *The Lancet* 395, no. 10221 (2020): 384–388, https://doi.org/10.1016/s0140-6736(19)32682-0.

136 Moore et al., 'Evolution of an HIV Glycan-Dependent Broadly Neutralizing Antibody Epitope'.

CHAPTER 7 Vaccination and the eradication of disease

137 WHO, 'Immunization', 5 December 2019, accessed 30 May 2023, https://www.who.int/news-room/facts-in-pictures/detail/immunizationq.

138 Saad B. Omer, Walter A. Orenstein and Jeffrey P. Koplan, 'Go Big and Go Fast – Vaccine Refusal and Disease Eradication', *New England Journal of Medicine* 368, no. 15 (2013): 1374–1376, https://doi.org/10.1056/nejmp1300765.

139 Donald R. Hopkins, 'Disease Eradication', *New England Journal of Medicine* 368, no. 1 (2013): 54–63, https://doi.org/10.1056/nejmra1200391.

140 Patrick Berche, 'Life and Death of Smallpox', *La Presse Médicale* 51, no. 3 (2022): 104117, https://doi.org/10.1016/j.lpm.2022.104117.

141 CDC, 'Smallpox', 12 July 2017, https://www.cdc.gov/smallpox/index.html#:~:text=In%201980%2C%20the%20World%20Health,occurring%20smallpox%20have%20happened%20since, accessed 30 May 2023.

142 William H. Foege, *House on Fire: The Fight to Eradicate Smallpox* (Berkeley: University of California Press, 2011).

143 Frank Fenner et al., *Smallpox and Its Eradication* (Geneva: World Health Organization, 1988), https://apps.who.int/iris/handle/10665/39485/, accessed 30 May 2023.

144 Monica Rimmer, 'How Smallpox Claimed Its Final Victim', *BBC News*, 10 August 2018, https://www.bbc.com/news/uk-england-birmingham-45101091, accessed 30 May 2023.

145 Karl Simpson et al., 'Human Monkeypox: After 40 Years, an Unintended Consequence of Smallpox Eradication', *Vaccine* 38, no. 33 (2020): 5077–5081, https://doi.org/10.1016/j.vaccine.2020.04.062.

146 Eric Dumonteil, Claudia Herrera and Gilberto Sabino-Santos, 'Monkeypox Virus Evolution before 2022 Outbreak', *Emerging Infectious Diseases* 29, no. 2 (2023): 451–453, https://doi.org/10.3201/eid2902.220962.

147 WHO, *2022–23 Mpox (Monkeypox) Outbreak: Global Trends*, 2023, accessed 30 May 2023, https://worldhealthorg.shinyapps.io/mpx_global/.

148 Ifedayo Adetifa et al., 'Mpox Neglect and the Smallpox Niche: A Problem for Africa, a Problem for the World', *The Lancet* 401, no. 10390 (2023): 1822–1824, https://doi.org/10.1016/s0140-6736(23)00588-3.

149 Over and above the polio vaccination component of the routine childhood vaccination schedule.

150 Leslie Roberts, 'Global Polio Eradication Falters in the Final Stretch', *Science* 367, no. 6473 (2020): 14–15, https://doi.org/10.1126/science.367.6473.14.

151 Bruce Aylward and Rudolf Tangermann, 'The Global Polio Eradication Initiative: Lessons Learned and Prospects for Success', *Vaccine* 29 (2011): D80–D85, https://doi.org/10.1016/j.vaccine.2011.10.005.

152 Philip Minor, 'Vaccine-Derived Poliovirus (VDPV): Impact on Poliomyelitis Eradication', *Vaccine* 27, no. 20 (2009): 2649–2652, https://doi.org/10.1016/j.vaccine.2009.02.071.

153 Marita Zimmermann, Brittany Hagedorn and Hil Lyons, 'Projection of Costs of Polio Eradication Compared to Permanent Control', *The Journal of Infectious Diseases* 221, no. 4 (2019): 561–565, https://doi.org/10.1093/infdis/jiz488.

154 GPEI, *Polio News*, May 2023, https://polioeradication.org/wp-content/uploads/2023/05/polio-news-may2023-en.pdf, accessed 30 May 2023.

155 Omer, Orenstein and Koplan, 'Go Big'.

156 Sophie Cousins, 'Pushing for Polio Eradication', *The Lancet* 399, no. 10340 (2022): 2004–2005, https://doi.org/10.1016/s0140-6736(22)00973-4.

157 Fenner equally famously predicted that humans could be extinct within 100 years, because of overpopulation, environmental destruction and climate change; Isao Arita, Miyuki Nakane and Frank Fenner, 'Is Polio Eradication Realistic?' *Science* 312, no. 5775 (2006): 852–854, https://doi.org/10.1126/science.1124959.

158 Zimmermann, Hagedorn and Lyons, 'Projection of Costs of Polio Eradication'.

159 James O. Lloyd-Smith, 'Vacated Niches, Competitive Release and the Community Ecology of Pathogen Eradication', *Philosophical Transactions of the Royal Society B: Biological Sciences* 368, no. 1623 (2013): 1–12, https://doi.org/10.1098/rstb.2012.0150.

160 Lloyd-Smith, 'Vacated Niches'.

161 World Health Organization, '34th Meeting of the International Task Force or Disease Eradication, 19–20 September 2022', accessed 30 May 2023, https://www.who.int/publications-detail-redirect/who-wer9804-41-50.

162 Wilson Smith, Christopher Howard Andrewes and Patrick Playfair Laidlaw, 'A Virus Obtained from Influenza Patients', *The Lancet* 222, no. 5732 (1933): 66–68, https://doi.org/10.1016/s0140-6736(00)78541-2.

163 Jasper Fuk-Woo Chan et al., 'A Familial Cluster of Pneumonia Associated with the 2019 Novel Coronavirus Indicating Person-to-Person Transmission: A Study of a Family Cluster', *The Lancet* 395, no. 10223 (2020): 514–523, https://doi.org/10.1016/s0140-6736(20)30154-9.

164 Kristian G. Andersen et al., 'The Proximal Origin of SARS-COV-2', *Nature Medicine* 26, no. 4 (2020): 450–452, https://doi.org/10.1038/s41591-020-0820-9.

165 Frederick A. Murphy, 'Emerging Zoonoses', *Emerging Infectious Diseases* 4, no. 3 (1998): 429–435, https://doi.org/10.3201/eid0403.980324.

166 Kaw Bing Chua, 'Nipah Virus Outbreak in Malaysia', *Journal of Clinical Virology* 26, no. 3 (2003): 265–275, https://doi.org/10.1016/s1386-6532(02)00268-8.

167 El Niño describes the largest climatic fluctuations on earth, as a result of the periodic warming of the oceans every few years.

168 Muge Cevik et al., 'SARS-COV-2, SARS-COV, and MERS-COV Viral Load Dynamics, Duration of Viral Shedding, and Infectiousness: A Systematic Review and Meta-analysis', *The Lancet Microbe* 2, no. 1 (2021): e13–e22, https://doi.org/10.1016/s2666-5247(20)30172-5.

169 Alfred W. Crosby, 'Virgin Soil Epidemics as a Factor in the Aboriginal Depopulation in America', *The William and Mary Quarterly* 33, no. 2 (1976): 289, https://doi.org/10.2307/1922166.

170 Philip Lawrence et al., 'Human Transmission of Ebola Virus', *Current Opinion in Virology* 22 (2017): 51–58, https://doi.org/10.1016/j.coviro.2016.11.013.

171 Howard Phillips, *Epidemics: The Story of South Africa's Five Most Lethal Human Diseases* (Athens: Ohio University Press, 2012).

172 Smith, Andrewes and Laidlaw, 'A Virus'.

173 Saloni Dattani and Fiona Spooner, 'How Many People Die from the Flu?' *Our World in Data*, 2022, https://ourworldindata.org/influenza-deaths, accessed 31 May 2023.

174 Anni McLeod, 'The Economics of Avian Influenza', in *Avian Influenza*, ed. David E. Swayne, 537–560 (Ames, IA: Wiley Blackwell, 2017).

175 Marietjie Venter et al., 'Risk of Human Infections with Highly Pathogenic H5N2 and Low Pathogenic H7N1 Avian Influenza Strains during Outbreaks in Ostriches in South Africa', *The Journal of Infectious Diseases* 216, suppl. 4 (2017): S512–S519, https://doi.org/10.1093/infdis/jix018.

176 Douglas Jordan, *The Deadliest Flu: The Complete Story of the Discovery and Reconstruction of the 1918 Pandemic Virus*, Centers for Disease Control and Prevention, 2019, https://www.cdc.gov/flu/pandemic-resources/reconstruction-1918-virus.html, accessed 31 May 2023.

177 Terrence M. Tumpey et al., 'Characterization of the Reconstructed 1918 Spanish Influenza Pandemic Virus', *Science* 310, no. 5745 (2005): 77–80, https://doi.org/10.1126/science.1119392.

178 Worldometer, *COVID-19 Coronavirus Pandemic: Coronavirus Cases*, 2023, https://www.worldometers.info/coronavirus/, accessed 31 May 2023.

179 Sonja J. Olsen et al., 'Decreased Influenza Activity during the COVID-19 Pandemic – United States, Australia, Chile, and South Africa', 2020, *Morbidity*

and Mortality Weekly Report 69, no. 37 (2020): 1305–1309. https://www.cdc.gov/mmwr/volumes/69/wr/mm6937a6.htm, accessed 31 May 2023.

180 Chan et al., 'A Familial Cluster'.

181 Aled M. Edwards et al., 'Stopping Pandemics before They Start: Lessons Learned from SARS-COV-2', *Science* 375, no. 6585 (2022): 1133–1139, https://doi.org/10.1126/science.abn1900.

182 Fatima Hassan, Gavin Yamey and Kamran Abbasi, 'Profiteering from Vaccine Inequity: A Crime against Humanity?' *BMJ* 374 (2021): n2027, https://doi.org/10.1136/bmj.n2027.

183 Oliver J. Watson et al., 'Global Impact of the First Year of COVID-19 Vaccination: A Mathematical Modelling Study', *The Lancet Infectious Diseases* 22, no. 9 (2022): 1293–1302, https://doi.org/10.1016/s1473-3099(22)00320-6.

184 Jie Cui, Fang Li and Zheng-Li Shi, 'Origin and Evolution of Pathogenic Coronaviruses', *Nature Reviews Microbiology* 17, no. 3 (2019): 181–192, https://doi.org/10.1038/s41579-018-0118-9.

185 Andersen et al., 'Proximal Origin'; Robert F. Garry, 'The Evidence Remains Clear: SARS-COV-2 Emerged Via the Wildlife Trade', *Proceedings of the National Academy of Sciences* 119, no. 47 (2022): 1–5, https://doi.org/10.1073/pnas.2214427119.

186 Peng Zhou and Zheng-Li Shi, 'SARS-COV-2 Spillover Events', *Science* 371, no. 6525 (2021): 120–122, https://doi.org/10.1126/science.abf6097.

187 Lytras et al., 'The Animal Origin'.

188 Garry, 'The Evidence Remains Clear'.

189 David A. Relman, 'To Stop the Next Pandemic, We Need to Unravel the Origins of COVID-19', *Proceedings of the National Academy of Sciences* 117, no. 47 (2020): 29246–29248, https://doi.org/10.1073/pnas.2021133117.

190 Jennie S. Lavine, Ottar N. Bjornstad and Rustom Antia, 'Immunological Characteristics Govern the Changing Severity of COVID-19 during the Transition to Endemicity', *Science* 371 (2020): 741–745, https://doi.org/10.1101/2020.09.03.20187856.

191 Ramon Lorenzo-Redondo, Egon A. Ozer and Judd F. Hultquist. 'COVID-19: Is Omicron Less Lethal Than Delta?' *BMJ* 378 (2022): o1806, https://doi.org/10.1136/bmj.o1806.

192 Eleanor G. Bentley et al., 'SARS-COV-2 Omicron-B.1.1.529 Variant Leads to Less Severe Disease than Pango B and Delta Variants Strains in a Mouse Model of Severe COVID-19', *BioRxiv* (2021) [Preprint], https://doi.org/10.1101/2021.12.26.474085.

193 Jeremy Bingham et al., 'Estimates of Prevalence of Anti-SARS-Cov-2 Antibodies among Blood Donors in South Africa in March 2022', *Research Square* (2022) [Preprint], https://doi.org/10.21203/rs.3.rs-1687679/v2.

194 Jefferson M. Jones et al., 'Updated US Infection- and Vaccine-Induced SARS-COV-2 Seroprevalence Estimates Based on Blood Donations, July 2020–December 2021', *JAMA* 328, no. 3 (2022): 298–300, https://doi.org/10.1001/jama.2022.9745.

195 Ioannidis et al., 'Massive Covidization'.

196 Levy et al., 'Wastewater Surveillance'.

197 Lawrence O. Gostin et al., 'Human Rights and the COVID-19 Pandemic: A Retrospective and Prospective Analysis', *The Lancet* 401, no. 10371 (2023): 154–168, https://doi.org/10.1016/s0140-6736(22)01278-8.

198 Caroline E. Wagner et al., 'Vaccine Nationalism and the Dynamics and Control of SARS-COV-2', *Science* 373 (2021): 1–10, https://doi.org/10.1101/2021.06.02.21258229.

199 Hassan, Yamey and Abbasi, 'Profiteering from Vaccine Inequity'.
200 Francois W.D. Venter et al., 'South Africa Should Be Using All the COVID-19 Vaccines Available to It – Urgently', *South African Medical Journal* 111, no. 5 (2021): 390–392, https://doi.org/10.7196/samj.2021.v111i5.15716.
201 Abdool Karim and De Oliveira, 'New SARS-COV-2 Variants'.
202 Barry D. Schoub, 'Dial Down the Rhetoric over COVID Vaccines', *South African Medical Journal* 111, no. 6 (2021): 522–523, https://doi.org/https://doi.org/10.7196/SAMJ.2021.v111i615740.
203 Jerald Sadoff et al., 'Safety and Efficacy of Single-Dose Ad26.COV2.S Vaccine against COVID-19', *New England Journal of Medicine* 384, no. 23 (2021): 2187–2201, https://doi.org/10.1056/nejmoa2101544.

EPILOGUE

204 WHO, 'Infodemic', 2020, accessed 2 August 2023, https://www.who.int/health-topics/infodemic?utmsource=substack&utmmedium=email#tab=tab1.
205 Nathan C. Lo and Peter J. Hotez, 'Public Health and Economic Consequences of Vaccine Hesitancy for Measles in the United States', *JAMA Pediatrics* 171, no. 9 (2017): 887–892, https://doi.org/10.1001/jamapediatrics.2017.1695.
206 Alberto Giubilini, 'Vaccination Ethics', *British Medical Bulletin* 137, no. 1 (2020): 4–12, https://doi.org/10.1093/bmb/ldaa036.
207 Romain Muller, 'Systemic Toxicity of Chloroquine and Hydroxychloroquine: Prevalence, Mechanisms, Risk Factors, Prognostic and Screening Possibilities', *Rheumatology International* 41, no. 7 (2021): 1189–1902, https://doi.org/10.1007/s00296-021-04868-6.
208 Sera Tort and Agustín Ciapponi, 'For Adults with Mild or Moderate to Severe Symptomatic COVID-19, What Are the Effects of Ivermectin?' *Cochrane Clinical Answers* [Preprint], 2022, https://doi.org/10.1002/cca.4030.
209 Temple et al., 'Toxic Effects from Ivermectin Use'.
210 Bianca Nogrady, '"I Hope You Die": How the COVID Pandemic Unleashed Attacks on Scientists', *Nature* 598, no. 7880 (2021): 250–253, https://doi.org/10.1038/d41586-021-02741-x.
211 Sean Fleming, 'These Are the World's Greatest Threats in 2021', *World Economic Forum*, 2021, https://www.weforum.org/agenda/2021/01/these-are-the-worlds-greatest-threats-2021/, accessed 1 August 2023.
212 Simon Beard and Lauren Holt, 'What Are the Biggest Threats to Humanity?' *BBC News*, 15 February 2019, https://www.bbc.com/news/world-47030233, accessed 1 August 2023.
213 Lisa Cox, 'Ten Threats to Humanity's Survival Identified in Australian Report Calling for Action', *The Guardian*, 2020, https://www.theguardian.com/world/2020/apr/22/ten-threats-to-humanitys-survival-identified-in-australian-report-calling-for-action, accessed 1 August 2023.
214 Loraine Balita-Centeno, '10 of the Greatest Threats to Human Life Around the World Today', *WorldAtlas*, 17 June 2020, https://www.worldatlas.com/articles/10-of-the-greatest-threats-to-human-life-around-the-world-today.html, accessed 1 August 2023.

215 Worldometer, 'Coronavirus Cases'.

216 Nouriel Roubini, 'This Is What the Economic Fallout from Coronavirus Could Look Like', *World Economic Forum*, 6 April 2020, https://www.weforum.org/agenda/2020/04/depression-global-economy-coronavirus/, accessed 1 August 2023.

217 Channing Arndt et al., 'Impact of COVID-19 on the South African Economy – An Initial Analysis', SA-TIED Working Paper 111, 2020, accessed 1 August 2023, https://sa tied.wider.unu.edu/sites/default/files/pdf/SA-TIED-WP-111.pdf.

BIBLIOGRAPHY

Abdool Karim, Salim S. and Tulio de Oliveira. 'New SARS-COV-2 Variants – Clinical, Public Health, and Vaccine Implications'. *New England Journal of Medicine* 384, no. 19 (2021): 1866–1868. https://doi.org/10.1056/nejmc2100362.

Adetifa, Ifedayo, Jean-Jacques Muyembe, Daniel G. Bausch and David L. Heymann. 'Mpox Neglect and the Smallpox Niche: A Problem for Africa, a Problem for the World'. *The Lancet* 401, no. 10390 (2023): 1822–1824. https://doi.org/10.1016/s0140-6736(23)00588-3.

African National Congress. *A National Health Plan for South Africa*. Johannesburg: African National Congress, 1994.

AIDS Advisory Panel. *Presidential AIDS Advisory Panel Report*. 2001. https://www.gov.za/sites/default/files/gcis_document/201409/aidspanelpdf0.pdf. Accessed 29 May 2023.

Alexander, Leonard L. 'East London Complaint: Further Statement by the Minister'. *South African Medical Journal* 29, no. 36 (1955): 848–849.

Alibek, Ken. *Biohazard*. London: Cornerstone Digital, 2008.

Andersen, Kristian G., Andrew Rambaut, W. Ian Lipkin, Edward C. Holmes and Robert F. Garry. 'The Proximal Origin of SARS-COV-2'. *Nature Medicine* 26, no. 4 (2020): 450–452. https://doi.org/10.1038/s41591-020-0820-9.

Arita, Isao, Miyuki Nakane and Frank Fenner. 'Is Polio Eradication Realistic?' *Science* 312, no. 5775 (2006): 852–854. https://doi.org/10.1126/science.1124959.

Arndt, Channing, Davies, Rob; Gabriel, Sherwin; Harris, Laurence; Makrelov, Konstantin; Modise, Boipuso; Robinson, Sherman; Simbanegavi, Witness; van Seventer, Dirk; and Anderson, Lillian. 'Impact of COVID-19 on the South African Economy – An Initial Analysis'. SA-TIED Working Paper 111, 2020. Accessed 1 August 2023, https://sa-tied.wider.unu.edu/sites/default/files/pdf/SA-TIED-WP-111.pdf.

Ayles, Helen, Linda Mureithi and Musonda Simwinga. 'The State of Tuberculosis in South Africa: What Does the First National Tuberculosis Prevalence Survey Teach Us?' *The Lancet Infectious Diseases* 22, no. 8 (2022): 1094–1096. https://doi.org/10.1016/s1473-3099(22)00286-9.

Aylward, Bruce and Rudolf Tangermann. 'The Global Polio Eradication Initiative: Lessons Learned and Prospects for Success'. *Vaccine* 29 (2011): D80–D85. https://doi.org/10.1016/j.vaccine.2011.10.005.

Balawanth, Ryleen, Inessa Ba, Bheki Qwabe, Laura Gast, Rajendra Maharaj, Jaishree Raman, Rebecca Graffy, Mbavhalelo Shandukani and Devanand Moonasar. 'Assessing Kwa-Zulu-Natal's Progress Towards Malaria Elimination and Its Readiness for Sub-national Verification'. *Malaria Journal* 18, no. 1 (2019): 108. https://doi.org/10.1186/s12936-019-2739-5.

Balita-Centeno, Loraine. '10 of the Greatest Threats to Human Life Around the World Today'. *WorldAtlas*, 17 June 2020. https://www.worldatlas.com/articles/10-of-the-greatest-threats-to-human-life-around-the-world-today.html. Accessed 1 August 2023.

Barré-Sinoussi, Françoise, Jean Claude Chermann, Françoise Rey, Marie-Therese Nugeyre, Solange Chamaret, Jacqueline Gruest, Charles Dauguet et al. 'Isolation of a T-lymphotropic Retrovirus from a Patient at Risk for Acquired Immune Deficiency Syndrome (AIDS)'. *Science* 220, no. 4599 (1983): 868–871. https://doi.org/10.1126/science.6189183.

Beard, Simon and Lauren Holt. 'What Are the Biggest Threats to Humanity?' *BBC News*, 15 February 2019. Accessed 1 August 2023. https://www.bbc.com/news/world-47030233.

Bekker, Linda-Gail, Roger Tatoud, Francois Dabis, Mark Feinberg, Pontiano Kaleebu, Mary Marovich, Thumbi Ndung'u et al. 'The Complex Challenges of HIV Vaccine Development Require Renewed and Expanded Global Commitment'. *The Lancet* 395, no. 10221 (2020): 384–388. https://doi.org/10.1016/s0140-6736(19)32682-0.

Bentley, Eleanor G., Adam Kirby, Parul Sharma, Anja Kipar, Daniele F. Mega, Chloe Bramwell, Rebekah Penrice-Randal et al. 'SARS-COV-2 Omicron-B.1.1.529 Variant Leads to Less Severe Disease than Pango B and Delta Variants Strains in a Mouse Model of Severe COVID-19'. *BioRxiv* (2021) [Preprint]. https://doi.org/10.1101/2021.12.26.474085.

Berche, Patrick. 'Life and Death of Smallpox'. *La Presse Médicale* 51, no. 3 (2022): 104117. https://doi.org/10.1016/j.lpm.2022.104117.

Bingham, Jeremy, Russel Cable, Charl Coleman, Tanya Nadia Glatt, Eduard Grebe, Laurette Mhlanga, Cynthia Nyano et al. 'Estimates of Prevalence of Anti-SARS-Cov-2 Antibodies among Blood Donors in South Africa in March 2022'. *Research Square* (2022) [Preprint]. https://doi.org/10.21203/rs.3.rs-1687679/v2.

Bloland, Peter, Patricia Simone, Brent Burkholder, Laurence Slutsker and Kevin M. de Cock. 'The Role of Public Health Institutions in Global Health System Strengthening Efforts: The US CDC's Perspective'. *PLoS Medicine* 9, no. 4 (2012): 1–5. https://doi.org/10.1371/journal.pmed.1001199.

Boon, Sarah. '21st Century Science Overload'. Canadian Science Publishing, 7 January 2018 (blog). Accessed 22 May 2023. http://blog.cdnsciencepub.com/21st-century-science-overload/.

Broder, Samuel and Robert C. Gallo. 'A Pathogenic Retrovirus (HTLV-III) Linked to AIDS'. *New England Journal of Medicine* 311, no. 20 (1984): 1292–1297. https://doi.org/10.1056/nejm198411153112006.

Budgell, Eric, Adam L. Cohen, Jo McAnerney, Sibongile Walaza, Shabir A. Madhi, Lucille Blumberg, Halima Dawood et al. 'Evaluation of Two Influenza Surveillance Systems in South Africa'. *PLoS One* 10, no. 3 (2015): e0120226. https://doi.org/10.1371/journal.pone.0120226.

Burke, Ashley, Yael Dahan-Moss, Frances Duncan, Bheki Qwabe, Maureen Coetzee, Lizette Koekemoer and Basil Brooke. '*Anopheles parensis* Contributes to Residual Malaria Transmission in South Africa'. *Malaria Journal* 18, no. 1 (2019): 257. https://doi.org/10.1186/s12936-019-2889-5.

Cameron, Edwin and Nathan Geffen. *Witness to AIDS*. Grahamstown: South African Library for the Blind, 2006.

CDC (Centers for Disease Control and Prevention). 'Smallpox'. 12 July 2017. https://www.cdc.gov/smallpox/index.html#:~:text=In%201980%2C%20the%20World%20Health,occurring%20smallpox%20have%20happened%20since. Accessed 30 May 2023.

CDC. 'David J. Sencer CDC Musuem: Our History – Our Story'. 19 April 2023. https://www.cdc.gov/museum/history/our-story.html. Accessed 22 May 2023.

CDC. 'Kaposi's Sarcoma and *Pneumocystis* Pneumonia among Homosexual Men – New York City and California'. *Morbidity and Mortality Weekly Report* 30, no. 25 (1981): 305–308.

CDC. 'Marburg Virus Disease Outbreaks'. 9 June 2023. https://www.cdc.gov/vhf/marburg/outbreaks/chronology.html. Accessed 24 May 2023.

CDC. 'Moving Towards the UNAIDS 90-90-90 Targets'. 14 March 2019. https://www.cdc.gov/globalhealth/stories/2019/moving-towards-unaids.html. Accessed 29 May 2023.

CDC. '*Pneumocystis* Pneumonia – Los Angeles'. *Morbidity and Mortality Weekly Report* 30, no. 21 (1981): 250–252.

Cevik, Muge, Matthew Tate, Ollie Lloyd, Alberto Enrico Maraolo, Jenna Schafers and Antonia Ho. 'SARS-COV-2, SARS-COV, and MERS-COV Viral Load Dynamics, Duration of Viral Shedding, and Infectiousness: A Systematic Review and Meta-analysis'. *The Lancet Microbe* 2, no. 1 (2021): e13–e22. https://doi.org/10.1016/s2666-5247(20)30172-5.

Chan, Jasper Fuk-Woo, Shuofeng Yuan, Kin-Hang Kok, Kelvin Kai-Wang To, Hin Chu, Jin Yang, Fanfan Xing et al. 'A Familial Cluster of Pneumonia Associated with the 2019 Novel Coronavirus Indicating Person-to-Person Transmission: A Study of a Family Cluster'. *The Lancet* 395, no. 10223 (2020): 514–523. https://doi.org/10.1016/s0140-6736(20)30154-9.

Chen, Chaomei. *Mapping Scientific Frontiers: The Quest for Knowledge Visualization*. London: Springer, 2017.

Chigwedere, Pride, George R. Seage 3rd, Sofia Gruskin, Tun-Hou Lee and Max E. Essex. 'Estimating the Lost Benefits of Antiretroviral Drug Use in South Africa'. *JAIDS Journal of Acquired Immune Deficiency Syndromes* 49, no. 4 (2008): 410–415. https://doi.org/10.1097/qai.0b013e31818a6cd5.

Chua, Kaw Bing. 'Nipah Virus Outbreak in Malaysia'. *Journal of Clinical Virology* 26, no. 3 (2003): 265–275. https://doi.org/10.1016/s1386-6532(02)00268-8.

Clavel, François, Denise Guétard, Françoise Brun-Vézinet, Sophie Chamaret, Marie-Anne Rey, Maria Odette Santos-Ferreira, Anne G. Laurent et al. 'Isolation of a New Human Retrovirus from West African Patients with AIDS'. *Science* 233, no. 4761 (1986): 343–346. https://doi.org/10.1126/science.2425430.

Cohen, Mitchell L. 'Changing Patterns of Infectious Disease'. *Nature* 406, no. 6797 (2000): 762–767. https://doi.org/10.1038/35021206.

Colebunders, Robert, Antoine Tshomba, Maria D. Van Kerkhove, Daniel G. Bausch, Pat Campbell, Modeste Libande, Patricia Pirard et al. 'Marburg Hemorrhagic Fever in Durba and Watsa, Democratic Republic of the Congo: Clinical Documentation, Features of Illness, and Treatment'. *The Journal of Infectious Diseases* 196, suppl. 2 (2007): S148–S153. https://doi.org/10.1086/520543.

Coovadia, Hoosen, Rachel Jewkes, Peter Barron, David Sanders and Diane McIntyre. 'The Health and Health System of South Africa: Historical Roots of Current Public Health Challenges'. *The Lancet* 374, no. 9692 (2009): 817–834. https://doi.org/10.1016/s0140-6736(09)60951-x.

Cousins, Sophie. 'Pushing for Polio Eradication'. *The Lancet* 399, no. 10340 (2022): 2004–2005. https://doi.org/10.1016/s0140-6736(22)00973-4.

Cox, Lisa. 'Ten Threats to Humanity's Survival Identified in Australian Report Calling for Action'. *The Guardian*, 21 April 2020. https://www.theguardian.com/world/2020/apr/22/ten-threats-to-humanitys-survival-identified-in-australian-report-calling-for-action. Accessed 1 August 2023.

Crosby, Alfred W. 'Virgin Soil Epidemics as a Factor in the Aboriginal Depopulation in America'. *The William and Mary Quarterly* 33, no. 2 (1976): 289. https://doi.org/10.2307/1922166.

Cui, Jie, Fang Li and Zheng-Li Shi. 'Origin and Evolution of Pathogenic Coronaviruses'. *Nature Reviews Microbiology* 17, no. 3 (2019): 181–192. https://doi.org/10.1038/s41579-018-0118-9.

Dandalo, Leonard C., Alan Kemp, Lizette L. Koekemoer and Givemore Munhenga. 'Effect of Ionising (Gamma) Radiation on Female *Anopheles arabiensis*'. *Transactions of the Royal Society of Tropical Medicine and Hygiene* 111, no. 1 (2017): 38–40. https://doi.org/10.1093/trstmh/trx013.

Dattani, Saloni and Fiona Spooner. 'How Many People Die from the Flu?' *Our World in Data*, 2022. https://ourworldindata.org/influenza-deaths. Accessed 31 May 2023.

De Jesus, Erin Garcia. 'After 40 Years of AIDS, Here's Why We Still Don't Have an HIV Vaccine'. *Science News*, 4 June 2021.

Dietz, Patricia M., Amara Jambai, Janusz T. Paweska, Zabulon Yoti and Thomas G. Ksiazek. 'Epidemiology and Risk Factors for Ebola Virus Disease in Sierra Leone – 23 May 2014 to 31 January 2015'. *Clinical Infectious Diseases* 61, no. 11 (2015): 1648–1654.

Dumonteil, Eric, Claudia Herrera and Gilberto Sabino-Santos. 'Monkeypox Virus Evolution before 2022 Outbreak'. *Emerging Infectious Diseases* 29, no. 2 (2023): 451–453. https://doi.org/10.3201/eid2902.220962.

Edwards, Aled M., Ralph S. Baric, Erica Ollmann Saphire and Jeffrey B. Ulmer. 'Stopping Pandemics before They Start: Lessons Learned from SARS-COV-2'. *Science* 375, no. 6585 (2022): 1133–1139. https://doi.org/10.1126/science.abn1900.

Fenner, Frank, Donald A. Henderson, Isao Arita, Zdenek Ježek and Ivan Danilovich Ladnyi. *Smallpox and Its Eradication*. Geneva: World Health Organization, 1988. https://apps.who.int/iris/handle/10665/39485/. Accessed 30 May 2023.

Fleming, Sean. 'These Are the World's Greatest Threats in 2021'. *World Economic Forum*, 2021. https://www.weforum.org/agenda/2021/01/these-are-the-worlds-greatest-threats-2021/. Accessed 1 August 2023.

Foege, William H. *House on Fire: The Fight to Eradicate Smallpox*. Berkeley: University of California Press, 2011.

Frontline. 'Thabo Mbeki's Letter'. *Frontline: The Age of AIDS*, 2006. https://www.pbs.org/wgbh/pages/frontline/aids/docs/mbeki.html. Accessed 29 May 2023.

Garry, Robert F. 'The Evidence Remains Clear: SARS-COV-2 Emerged Via the Wildlife Trade'. *Proceedings of the National Academy of Sciences* 119, no. 47 (2022): 1–5. https://doi.org/10.1073/pnas.2214427119.

Gear, James H. 'Clinical Aspects of African Viral Hemorrhagic Fevers'. *Clinical Infectious Diseases* 11, suppl. 4 (1989). https://doi.org/10.1093/clinids/11.supplement_4.s777.

Gear, James H.S. *The History of the Poliomyelitis Research Foundation*. Johannesburg: The Poliomyelitis Research Foundation, 1996. https://doi.org/10.1093/cid/civ568.

Gear, James S., Graeme A. Cassel, John S. Gear, Brian Trappler, Lavinia Clausen, Anthony M. Meyers, Michael C. Kew et al. 'Outbreak of Marburg Virus Disease in Johannesburg'. *BMJ* 4, no. 5995 (1975): 489–493. https://doi.org/10.1136/bmj.4.5995.489.

George, Gavin, Cherie Cawood, Adrian Puren, David Khanyile, Annette Gerritsen, Kaymarlin Govender, Sean Beckett et al. 'Evaluating DREAMS HIV Prevention Interventions Targeting Adolescent Girls and Young Women in High HIV Prevalence Districts in South Africa: Protocol for a Cross-Sectional Study'. *BMC Women's Health* 20, no. 1 (2020): 7. https://doi.org/10.1186/s12905-019-0875-2.

Giubilini, Alberto. 'Vaccination Ethics'. *British Medical Bulletin* 137, no. 1 (2020): 4–12. https://doi.org/10.1093/bmb/ldaa036.

Gostin, Lawrence O., Eric A. Friedman, Sara Hossain, Joia Mukherjee, Saman Zia-Zarifi, Chelsea Clinton, Umunyana Rugege et al. 'Human Rights and the COVID-19 Pandemic: A Retrospective and Prospective Analysis'. *The Lancet* 401, no. 10371 (2023): 154–168. https://doi.org/10.1016/s0140-6736(22)01278-8.

Gould, Chandré, Peter I. Folb and Robert Berold, UN Institute for Disarmament Research, Centre for Conflict Resolution (Cape Town). *Project Coast: Apartheid's Chemical and Biological Warfare Programme*. Geneva: United Nations Publications, 2002.

GPEI (Global Polio Eradication Initiative). *Polio News*, May 2023. https://polioeradication.org/wp-content/uploads/2023/05/polio-news-may2023-en.pdf. Accessed 30 May 2023.

Hassan, Fatima, Gavin Yamey and Kamran Abbasi. 'Profiteering from Vaccine Inequity: A Crime against Humanity?' *BMJ* 374 (2021): n2027. https://doi.org/10.1136/bmj.n2027.

Hopkins, Donald R. 'Disease Eradication'. *New England Journal of Medicine* 368, no. 1 (2013): 54–63. https://doi.org/10.1056/nejmra1200391.

HSRC (Human Sciences Research Council). *South African National HIV Prevalence, Incidence, Behaviour and Communication Survey, 2008*, 2009. Accessed 10 November 2023, https://web.archive.org/web/20100522082857/http:/www.hsrc.ac.za/Document-3238.phtml.

Hunt, Gillian M., Johanna Ledwaba, Monalisa Kalimashe, Anna Salimo, Siyabonga Cibane, Beverly Singh, Adrian Puren, Natalie Exner Dean, Lynn Morris and Michael R. Jordan. 'Provincial and National Prevalence Estimates of Transmitted HIV-1 Drug Resistance in South Africa Measured Using Two WHO-Recommended Methods'. *Antiviral Therapy* 24, no. 3 (2018): 203–210. https://doi.org/10.3851/imp3294.

IANPHI (International Association of National Public Health Institutes). *Building Global Public Health Capacity*. 2023. https://www.ianphi.org/. Accessed 22 May 2023.

IANPHI. *Progress Report 2022*. 2022. https://www.ianphi.org/. Accessed 22 May 2023.

International Commission. 'Ebola Haemorrhagic Fever in Zaire, 1976'. *Bulletin of the World Health Organization* 56, no. 2 (1978): 271–293.

Ioannidis, John P.A., Eran Bendavid, Maia Salholz-Hillel and Jeroen Baas. 'Massive Covidization of Research Citations and the Citation Elite'. *Proceedings of the National*

Academy of Sciences 119, no. 28 (2022): e2204074119. https://doi.org/10.1073/pnas.2204074119.

Joint United Nations Programme on HIV/AIDS. *UNAIDS Data 2022*. 2022. https://www.unaids.org/sites/default/files/media_asset/data-book-2022_en.pdf. Accessed 28 May 2023.

Jones, Jefferson M., Jean D. Opsomer, Mars Stone, Tina Benoit, Robyn A. Ferg, Susan L. Stramer and Michael P. Busch. 'Updated US Infection- and Vaccine-Induced SARS-COV-2 Seroprevalence Estimates Based on Blood Donations, July 2020–December 2021'. *JAMA* 328, no. 3 (2022): 298–300. https://doi.org/10.1001/jama.2022.9745.

Jordan, Douglas. *The Deadliest Flu: The Complete Story of the Discovery and Reconstruction of the 1918 Pandemic Virus*. Centers for Disease Control and Prevention, 2019. https://www.cdc.gov/flu/pandemic-resources/reconstruction-1918-virus.html. Accessed 31 May 2023.

Kharsany, Ayesha B.M., Cherie Cawood, David Khanyile, Lara Lewis, Anneke Grobler, Adrian Puren, Kaymarlin Govender et al. 'Community-Based HIV Prevalence in KwaZulu-Natal, South Africa: Results of a Cross-Sectional Household Survey'. *The Lancet HIV* 5, no. 8 (2018): e427–e437. https://doi.org/10.1016/s2352-3018(18)30104-8.

Klein, Aaron E. *Trial by Fury: The Polio Vaccine Controversy*. New York: Scribner, 1972.

Langmuir, Alexander D. 'The Surveillance of Communicable Diseases of National Importance'. *New England Journal of Medicine* 268, no. 4 (1963): 182–192. https://doi.org/10.1056/nejm196301242680405.

Lavine, Jennie S., Ottar N. Bjornstad and Rustom Antia. 'Immunological Characteristics Govern the Changing Severity of COVID-19 during the Transition to Endemicity'. *Science* 371 (2020): 741–745. https://doi.org/10.1101/2020.09.03.20187856.

Lawrence, Philip, Nicolas Danet, Olivier Reynard, Valentina Volchkova and Viktor Volchkov. 'Human Transmission of Ebola Virus'. *Current Opinion in Virology* 22 (2017): 51–58. https://doi.org/10.1016/j.coviro.2016.11.013.

Levy, Joshua I., Kristian G. Andersen, Rob Knight and Smruthi Karthikeyan. 'Wastewater Surveillance for Public Health'. *Science* 379, no. 6627 (2023): 26–27. https://doi.org/10.1126/science.ade2503.

Lippman, Sheri A., Alison M. El Ayadi, Jessica S. Grignon, Adrian Puren, Teri Liegler, W. D. Francois Venter, Mary J. Ratlhagana et al. 'Improvements in the South African HIV Care Cascade: Findings on 90-90-90 Targets from Successive Population-Representative Surveys in North West Province'. *Journal of the International AIDS Society* 22, no. 6 (2019). https://doi.org/10.1002/jia2.25295.

Lloyd-Smith, James O. 'Vacated Niches, Competitive Release and the Community Ecology of Pathogen Eradication'. *Philosophical Transactions of the Royal Society B: Biological Sciences* 368, no. 1623 (2013): 1–12. https://doi.org/10.1098/rstb.2012.0150.

Lo, Nathan C. and Peter J. Hotez. 'Public Health and Economic Consequences of Vaccine Hesitancy for Measles in the United States'. *JAMA Pediatrics* 171, no. 9 (2017): 887–892. https://doi.org/10.1001/jamapediatrics.2017.1695.

Lorenzo-Redondo, Ramon, Egon A. Ozer and Judd F. Hultquist. 'COVID-19: Is Omicron Less Lethal Than Delta?' *BMJ* 378 (2022): o1806. https://doi.org/10.1136/bmj.o1806.

Lytras, Spyros, Wei Xia, Joseph Hughes, Xiaowei Jiang and David L. Robertson. 'The Animal Origin of SARS-COV-2'. *Science* 373, no. 6558 (2021): 968–970. https://doi.org/10.1126/science.abh0117.

Mackenzie, John S. and Martyn Jeggo. 'The One Health Approach – Why Is It So Important?' *Tropical Medicine and Infectious Disease* 4, no. 2 (2019): 88–91. https://doi.org/10.3390/tropicalmed4020088.

Makgoba, Malegapuru W. 'HIV/AIDS: The Peril of Pseudoscience'. *Science* 288, no. 5469 (2000): 1171. https://doi.org/10.1126/science.288.5469.1171.

Malan, Marais. *In Quest of Health: The South African Institute for Medical Research 1912–1973*. Johannesburg: Lowry Publishers, 1988.

Mashatola, Thabo, Cyrille Ndo, Lizette L. Koekemoer, Leonard C. Dandalo, Oliver R. Wood, Lerato Malakoane, Yacouba Poumachu et al. 'A Review on the Progress of Sex-Separation Techniques for Sterile Insect Technique Applications against *Anopheles arabiensis*'. *Parasites & Vectors* 11, no. S2 (2018). https://doi.org/10.1186/s13071-018-3219-4.

Mbunkah, Herbert A., Silvia Bertagnolio, Raph L. Hamers, Gillian Hunt, Seth Inzaule, Tobias F. Rinke de Wit, Roger Paredes et al. 'Low-Abundance Drug-Resistant HIV-1 Variants in Antiretroviral Drug-Naive Individuals: A Systematic Review of Detection Methods, Prevalence, and Clinical Impact'. *The Journal of Infectious Diseases* 221, no. 10 (2019): 1584–1597. https://doi.org/10.1093/infdis/jiz650.

McAnerney, Johanna M., Sylvia Johnson and Barry D. Schoub. 'Surveillance of Respiratory Viruses: A 10-Year Laboratory-Based Study'. *South African Medical Journal* 84, no. 8 Pt 1 (1994): 473–477.

McLeod, Anni. 'The Economics of Avian Influenza'. In *Avian Influenza*, edited by David E. Swayne, 537–560. Ames, IA: Wiley Blackwell, 2017.

McNutt, Marcia and Michael M. Crow. 'Enhancing Trust in Science and Democracy in an Age of Misinformation'. *Issues in Science and Technology* 29, no. 3 (2023): 18–20. https://doi.org/10.58875/fabl6884.

Metz, Jack. *South Africa's Health Sentinel: The South African Institute for Medical Research. 1974 to 1999.* Johannesburg: Adler Museum of Medicine, 2017.

Metz, Jack and Barry D. Schoub. 'James Gear – An Appreciation'. *South African Medical Journal* 70, no. 4 (1986): 6–7.

Michaud, Catherine M. 'Global Burden of Infectious Diseases'. *Encyclopedia of Microbiology* (2009): 444–454. https://doi.org/10.1016/b978-012373944-5.00185-1.

Minor, Philip. 'Vaccine-Derived Poliovirus (VDPV): Impact on Poliomyelitis Eradication'. *Vaccine* 27, no. 20 (2009): 2649–2652. https://doi.org/10.1016/j.vaccine.2009.02.071.

Moore, Penny L., Elin S. Gray, C. Kurt Wibmer, Jinal N. Bhiman, Molati Nonyane, Daniel J. Sheward, Tandile Hermanus et al. 'Evolution of an HIV Glycan-Dependent Broadly Neutralizing Antibody Epitope Through Immune Escape'. *Nature Medicine* 18, no. 11 (2012): 1688–1692. https://doi.org/10.1038/nm.2985.

Morgan, Oliver W., Philip Abdelmalik, Enrique Perez-Gutierrez, Ibrahima Socé Fall, Masaya Kato, Esther Hamblion, Tamano Matsui et al. 'How Better Pandemic and Epidemic Intelligence Will Prepare the World for Future Threats'. *Nature Medicine* 28, no. 8 (2022): 1526–1528. https://doi.org/10.1038/s41591-022-01900-5.

Muller, Romain. 'Systemic Toxicity of Chloroquine and Hydroxychloroquine: Prevalence, Mechanisms, Risk Factors, Prognostic and Screening Possibilities'. *Rheumatology International* 41, no. 7 (2021): 1189–1902. https://doi.org/10.1007/s00296-021-04868-6.

Murphy, Frederick A. 'Emerging Zoonoses'. *Emerging Infectious Diseases* 4, no. 3 (1998): 429–435. https://doi.org/10.3201/eid0403.980324.

Muyembe-Tamfum, Jean-Jacques, Mangala Kipasa, C. Kiyungu and Robert Colebunders. 'Ebola Outbreak in Kikwit, Democratic Republic of the Congo: Discovery and Control Measures'. *The Journal of Infectious Diseases* 179, suppl. 1 (1999): S259–S262. https://doi.org/10.1086/514302.

Myburgh, James. 'The Virodene Affair (I)'. *Politicsweb*, 17 September 2007. https://www.politicsweb.co.za/news-and-analysis/the-virodene-affair-i. Accessed 29 May 2023.

NICD (National Institute for Communicable Diseases). *The 2019 National Antenatal HIV Sentinel Survey (ANCHSS) Key Findings*. 30 April 2021. https://www.nicd.ac.za/wp-content/uploads/2021/11/Antenatal-survey-2019-reportFINAL27April21.pdf1. Accessed 24 May 2023.

NICD. 'TB Surveillance Dashboard and Other Resources'. 2019. https://www.nicd.ac.za/tb-surveillance-dashboard/. Accessed 23 May 2023.

Nogrady, Bianca. '"I Hope You Die": How the COVID Pandemic Unleashed Attacks on Scientists'. *Nature* 598, no. 7880 (2021): 250–253. https://doi.org/10.1038/d41586-021-02741-x.

Oliver, Shüné V. and Basil D. Brooke. 'The Effect of Elevated Temperatures on the Life History and Insecticide Resistance Phenotype of the Major Malaria Vector *Anopheles arabiensis* (Diptera: Culicidae)'. *Malaria Journal* 16, no. 1 (2017). https://doi.org/10.1186/s12936-017-1720-4.

Olsen, Sonja J., Eduardo Azziz-Baumgartner, Alicia P. Budd, Lynnette Brammer, Sheena Sullivan, Rodrigo F. Pineda, Cheryl Cohen and Alicia M. Fry. 'Decreased Influenza Activity during the COVID-19 Pandemic – United States, Australia, Chile, and South Africa, 2020'. *Morbidity and Mortality Weekly Report* 69, no. 37 (2020): 1305–1309. https://www.cdc.gov/mmwr/volumes/69/wr/mm6937a6.htm. Accessed 31 May 2023.

Omer, Saad B., Walter A. Orenstein and Jeffrey P. Koplan. 'Go Big and Go Fast – Vaccine Refusal and Disease Eradication'. *New England Journal of Medicine* 368, no. 15 (2013): 1374–1376. https://doi.org/10.1056/nejmp1300765.

O'Neill, Jim. 'Tackling Drug-Resistant Infections Globally: Final Report and Recommendations'. *The Review of Antimicrobial Resistance*, May 2016. https://amr-review.org/sites/default/files/160525Final%20paperwith%20cover.pdf. Accessed 23 May 2023.

Pawęska, Janusz T., Petrus Jansen van Vuuren, Alan Kemp, Nadia Storm, Antoinette A. Grobbelaar, Michael R. Wiley, Gustavo Palacios and Wanda Markotter. 'Marburg Virus Infection in Egyptian Rousette Bats, South Africa, 2013–2014'. *Emerging Infectious Diseases* 24, no. 6 (2018): 1134–1137. https://doi.org/10.3201/eid2406.172165.

Paweska, Janusz T., Petrus Jansen van Vuuren, Gunther H. Meier, Chantel le Roux, Ousman S. Conteh, Alan Kemp, Cardia Fourie et al. 'South African Ebola Diagnostic Response in Sierra Leone: A Modular High Biosafety Field Laboratory'. *PLOS Neglected Tropical Diseases* 11, no. 6 (2017): e0005665. https://doi.org/10.1371/journal.pntd.0005665.

Phillips, Howard. *Epidemics: The Story of South Africa's Five Most Lethal Human Diseases*. Athens: Ohio University Press, 2012.

———. *Plague, Pox and Pandemics: A Jacana Pocket History of Epidemics in South Africa*. Auckland Park: Jacana, 2012.

Piddock, Laura J.V. 'The Crisis of No New Antibiotics – What Is the Way Forward?' *The Lancet Infectious Diseases* 12, no. 3 (2012): 249–253. https://doi.org/10.1016/s1473-3099(11)70316-4.

'Prime Minister Warns of Global Threat of Antibiotic Resistance'. Press release, 2 July 2014. https://www.gov.uk/government/news/prime-minister-warns-of-global-threat-of-antibiotic-resistance. Accessed 23 May 2023.

Ras, Gerhardus Johannes, Ian William Simson, Ronald Anderson, Walter Prozesky and Theo Hamersma. 'Acquired Immunodeficiency Syndrome: A Report of 2 South African Cases'. *South African Medical Journal* 64 (1983): 140–142.

Reddy, Carl, Lazarus Kuonza, Hetani Ngobeni, Natalie T. Mayet, Timothy J. Doyle and Seymour Williams. 'South Africa Field Epidemiology Training Program: Developing and Building Applied Epidemiology Capacity, 2007–2016'. *BMC Public Health* 19, no. S3 (2019). https://doi.org/10.1186/s12889-019-6788-z.

Relman, David A. 'To Stop the Next Pandemic, We Need to Unravel the Origins of COVID-19'. *Proceedings of the National Academy of Sciences* 117, no. 47 (2020): 29246–29248. https://doi.org/10.1073/pnas.2021133117.

Rimmer, Monica. 'How Smallpox Claimed Its Final Victim'. *BBC News*, 10 August 2018. https://www.bbc.com/news/uk-england-birmingham-45101091. Accessed 30 May 2023.

Ritchie, Saloni, Fiona Spooner, Hannah Ritchie and Max Roser. 'Causes of Death'. *Our World in Data*, 2018. https://ourworldindata.org/causes-of-death. Accessed 22 May 2023.

Roberts, Leslie. 'Global Polio Eradication Falters in the Final Stretch'. *Science* 367, no. 6473 (2020): 14–15. https://doi.org/10.1126/science.367.6473.14.

Roubini, Nouriel. 'This Is What the Economic Fallout from Coronavirus Could Look Like'. *World Economic Forum*, 6 April 2020. https://www.weforum.org/agenda/2020/04/depression-global-economy-coronavirus/. Accessed 1 August 2023.

Sachs, Jeffrey D., Salim S. Abdool Karim, Lara Aknins, Joseph Allen, Kirsten Brosbøl, Francesca Colombo, Gabriela Cuevas et al. 'The Lancet Commission on Lessons for the Future from the COVID-19 Pandemic'. *The Lancet* 400, no. 10359 (2022): 1224–1280. https://doi.org/10.1016/50140-6736(22)01585-9.

Sadoff, Jerald, Glenda Gray, An Vandebosch, Vicky Cárdenas, Georgi Shukarev, Beatriz Grinsztejn, Paul A. Goepfert et al. 'Safety and Efficacy of Single-Dose Ad26.COV2.S Vaccine against COVID-19'. *New England Journal of Medicine* 384, no. 23 (2021): 2187–2201. https://doi.org/10.1056/nejmoa2101544.

Schoub, Barry D. 'Dial Down the Rhetoric over COVID Vaccines'. *South African Medical Journal* 111, no. 6 (2021): 522–523. https://doi.org/https://doi.org/10.7196/SAMJ.2021.v111i615740.

———. 'Estimation of the Total Size of the Human Immunodeficiency Virus and Hepatitis B Epidemics in South Africa'. *South African Medical Journal* 81 (1991): 63–66.

———. *Medical Virology: The Coming of Age: Inaugural Lecture*. Johannesburg: Witwatersrand University Press, 1983.

———. 'Professor HJ Koornhof – A Tribute and an Appreciation'. *South African Medical Journal* 97, no. 11 (2007): 1113.

Schoub, Barry D., Susan F. Lyons, Gillian M. McGillivray, Alan N. Smith, Sylvia Johnson and Ephraim L. Fisher. 'Absence of HIV Infection in Prostitutes and Women

Attending Sexually-Transmitted Disease Clinics in South Africa'. *Transactions of the Royal Society of Tropical Medicine and Hygiene* 81, no. 5 (1987): 874–875. https://doi.org/10.1016/0035-9203(87)90057-5.

Seung, Kwonjune J., Salmaan Keshavjee and Michael L. Rich. 'Multidrug-Resistant Tuberculosis and Extensively Drug-Resistant Tuberculosis'. *Cold Spring Harbor Perspectives in Medicine* 5, no. 9 (2015). https://doi.org/10.1101/cshperspect.a017863.

Sewlall, Nivesh H. and Janusz T. Paweska. 'Lujo Virus: Current Concepts'. *Virus Adaptation and Treatment* 9 (2017): 41–47. https://doi.org/10.2147/vaat.s113593.

Sharp, Paul M. and Beatrice H. Hahn. 'The Evolution of HIV-1 and the Origin of AIDS'. *Philosophical Transactions of the Royal Society B: Biological Sciences* 365, no. 1552 (2010): 2487–2494. https://doi.org/10.1098/rstb.2010.0031.

Sher, Rukhsana, Danilo Santos de Miranda, Jack Metz, Dennis Sifris, Susan F. Lyons and Barry D. Schoub. 'Lack of Evidence of HIV Infection in Drug Abusers at Present'. *South African Medical Journal* 70 (1986): 776–777.

Simbayi, Leikness, Nompumelelo Zungu, Khangelani Zuma et al. *South African National HIV Prevalence, Incidence, Behaviour and Communication Survey, 2017: Towards Achieving the UNAIDS 90-90-90 Targets*. Cape Town: HSRC Press, 2019.

Simpson, Karl, David Heymann, Colin S. Brown, W. John Edmunds, Jesper Elsgaard, Paul Fine, Hubertus Hochrein et al. 'Human Monkeypox: After 40 Years, an Unintended Consequence of Smallpox Eradication'. *Vaccine* 38, no. 33 (2020): 5077–5081. https://doi.org/10.1016/j.vaccine.2020.04.062.

Smith, Wilson, Christopher Howard Andrewes and Patrick Playfair Laidlaw. 'A Virus Obtained from Influenza Patients'. *The Lancet* 222, no. 5732 (1933): 66–68. https://doi.org/10.1016/s0140-6736(00)78541-2.

Spellberg, Brad. 'Dr. William H. Stewart: Mistaken or Maligned?' *Clinical Infectious Diseases* 47, no. 2 (2008): 294. https://doi.org/10.1086/589579.

Stats SA (Statistics South Africa). *Mid-Year Population Estimates 2021*. Statistical Release PO302. 2022. http://www.statssa.gov.za/publications/P0302/P03022021.pdf. Accessed 29 May 2023.

Swanepoel, Robert, Andrew James Shepherd, Patricia Anne Leman and Susan Patricia Shepherd. 'Investigations Following Initial Recognition of Crimean-Congo Haemorrhagic Fever in South Africa and the Diagnosis of 2 Further Cases'. *South African Medical Journal* 68, no. 9 (1985): 638–641.

Tegally, Houriiyah, Eduan Wilkinson, Marta Giovanetti, Arash Iranzadeh, Vagner Fonseca, Jennifer Giandhari, Deelan Doolabh et al. 'Detection of a SARS-COV-2 Variant of Concern in South Africa'. *Nature* 592, no. 7854 (2021): 438–443. https://doi.org/10.1038/s41586-021-03402-9.

Temple, Courtney, Ruby Hoang and Robert G. Hendrickson. 'Toxic Effects from Ivermectin Use Associated with Prevention and Treatment of COVID-19'. *New England Journal of Medicine* 385, no. 23 (2021): 2197–2198. https://doi.org/10.1056/nejmc2114907.

'The Durban Declaration'. *Nature* 406, no. 6791 (2000): 15–16. https://doi.org/10.1038/35017662.

Thomas, Juno, Nevashan Govender, Kerrigan M. McCarthy, Linda K. Erasmus, Timothy J. Doyle, Mushal Allam, Arshad Ismail et al. 'Outbreak of Listeriosis in South Africa Associated with Processed Meat'. *New England Journal of Medicine* 382, no. 7 (2020): 632–643. https://doi.org/10.1056/nejmoa1907462.

Thomson, Alastair. 'Mbeki Address: 13th International AIDS Conference'. *Scoop World*, 18 July 2000. https://www.scoop.co.nz/stories/WO0007/S00072/mbeki-address-13th-international-aids-conference.htm. Accessed 29 May 2023.

Tort, Sera and Agustín Ciapponi. 'For Adults with Mild or Moderate to Severe Symptomatic COVID-19, What Are the Effects of Ivermectin?' *Cochrane Clinical Answers* [Preprint], 2022. https://doi.org/10.1002/cca.4030.

Tshabalala-Msimang, Manto. 'Mbeki's Stand on AIDS was Dictated by African Realities'. *Sunday Independent*, 2 July 2000.

Tucker, Jonathan B. *Scourge: The Once and Future Threat of Smallpox*. New York: Grove Press, 2002.

Tumpey, Terrence M., Christopher F. Basler, Patricia V. Aguilar, Hui Zeng, Alicia Solórzano, David E. Swayne, Nancy J. Cox et al. 'Characterization of the Reconstructed 1918 Spanish Influenza Pandemic Virus'. *Science* 310, no. 5745 (2005): 77–80. https://doi.org/10.1126/science.1119392.

UNAIDS. *South Africa 2021*. 2021. https://www.unaids.org/en/regionscountries/countries/southafrica. Accessed 23 May 2023.

UNAIDS. 'Global HIV and AIDS Statistics – Fact Sheet'. 2021. https://www.unaids.org/en/resources/fact-sheet. Accessed 28 May 2023.

Unemo, Magnus and Robert A. Nicholas. 'Emergence of Multidrug-Resistant, Extensively Drug-Resistant and Untreatable Gonorrhea'. *Future Microbiology* 7, no. 12 (2012): 1401–1422. https://doi.org/10.2217/fmb.12.117.

Van Bambeke, Françoise, René R. Reinert, Peter C. Appelbaum, Paul M. Tulkens and Willy E. Peetermans. 'Multidrug-Resistant *Streptococcus pneumoniae* Infections: Current and Future Therapeutic Options'. *Drugs* 67, no. 16 (2007): 2355–2382. https://doi.org/10.2165/00003495-200767160-00005.

Venter, Francois W. D., Shabir A. Madhi, Jeremy Stephen Nel, Marc Mendelson, Alex van den Heever and Mosa Moshabela. 'South Africa Should Be Using All the COVID-19 Vaccines Available to It – Urgently'. *South African Medical Journal* 111, no. 5 (2021): 390–392. https://doi.org/10.7196/samj.2021.v111i5.15716.

Venter, Marietjie, Florette K. Treurnicht, Amelia Buys, Stefano Tempia, Rudo Samudzi, Johanna McAnerney, Charlene A. Jacobs, Juno Thomas and Lucille Blumberg. 'Risk of Human Infections with Highly Pathogenic H5N2 and Low Pathogenic H7N1 Avian Influenza Strains during Outbreaks in Ostriches in South Africa'. *The Journal of Infectious Diseases* 216, suppl. 4 (2017): S512–S519. https://doi.org/10.1093/infdis/jix018.

Viana, Raquel, Sikhulile Moyo, Daniel G. Amoako, Houriiyah Tegally, Cathrine Scheepers, Christian L. Althaus, Ugochukwu J. Anyaneji et al. 'Rapid Epidemic Expansion of the SARS-COV-2 Omicron Variant in Southern Africa'. *Nature* 603, no. 7902 (2022): 679–686. https://doi.org/10.1038/s41586-022-04411-y.

Wachter, Robert M. 'Nailing the Nuance on COVID-19'. *Science* 337 (2022): 243.

Wagner, Caroline E., Chadi M. Saad-Roy, Sinead E. Morris, Rachel E. Baker, Michael J. Mina, Jeremy Farrar, Edward C. Holmes et al. 'Vaccine Nationalism and the Dynamics and Control of SARS-COV-2'. *Science* 373 (2021): 1–10. https://doi.org/10.1101/2021.06.02.21258229.

Watkins, David I. 'The Vaccine Search Goes On'. *Scientific American* 299, no. 5 (2008): 69–76. https://doi.org/10.1038/scientificamerican1108-69.

Watson, Oliver J., Gregory Barnsley, Jaspreet Toor, Alexandra B. Hogan, Peter Winskill, Azra C. Ghani. 'Global Impact of the First Year of COVID-19 Vaccination: A Mathematical Modelling Study'. *The Lancet Infectious Diseases* 22, no. 9 (2022): 1293–1302. https://doi.org/10.1016/s1473-3099(22)00320-6.

Weyer, Jacqueline. 'Rabies in South Africa: Where Do We Stand in 2015?' *Southern African Journal of Infectious Diseases* 30, no. 2 (2015): 40–41. https://doi.org/10.108 0/16089677.2015.1094233.

Whitworth, Joe. 'Court Overturns Decision in Tiger Brands Listeria Case'. *Food Safety News*, 7 February 2022. https://www.foodsafetynews.com/2022/02/court-overturns-decision-in-tiger-brands-listeria-case/. Accessed 23 May 2023.

WHO (World Health Organization). *2022–23 Mpox (Monkeypox) Outbreak: Global Trends.* 2023. https://worldhealthorg.shinyapps.io/mpx_global/. Accessed 30 May 2023.

WHO. '34th Meeting of the International Task Force for Disease Eradication, 19–20 September 2022, World Health Organization'. *Weekly Epidemiological Record* no. 4 (27 January 2023). https://www.who.int/publications-detail-redirect/who-wer9804-41-50. Accessed 30 May 2023.

WHO. *Global Tuberculosis Report.* 2021. https://www.who.int/publications/i/item/9789 240037021. Accessed 15 January 2024.

WHO. *HIV Drug Resistance: Brief Report 2024.* https://www.who.int/publications/i/item/9789240086319. Accessed 26 April 2024.

WHO. 'Infodemic'. 2020. https://www.who.int/health-topics/infodemic?utm_source=substack&utm_medium=email#tab=tab_1. Accessed 2 August 2023.

WHO. 'Immunization'. 5 December 2019. https://www.who.int/news-room/facts-in-pictures/detail/immunizationq. Accessed 30 May 2023.

WHO. 'Recommended Composition of Influenza Virus Vaccines for Use in the 2023 Southern Hemisphere Influenza Season'. 23 September 2022. https://cdn.who.int/media/docs/default-source/influenza/who-influenza-recommendations/vcm-southern-hemisphere-recommendation-2023/202209recommendation.pdf?sfvrsn=83a26d503&download=true. Accessed 15 January 2024.

WHO. *World Malaria Report.* 6 December 2021. https://www.who.int/teams/global-malaria-programme/reports/world-malaria-report-2021. Accessed 1 March 2024.

Wikipedia. 'Lord Kelvin'. 2023. https://en.wikipedia.org/wiki/Lord_Kelvin. Accessed 20 August 2023.

Wikiquote. 'Albert A. Michelson'. 2023. https://en.wikiquote.org/wiki/AlbertA.Michelson. Accessed 20 August 2023.

Wilkinson, Amanda L., Ousmane M. Diop, Jaume Jorba, Tracie Gardner, Cynthia J. Snider and Jamal Ahmed. 'Surveillance to Track Progress Toward Polio Eradication – Worldwide, 2020–2021'. *Morbidity and Mortality Weekly Report* 71, no. 15 (2022): 538–544. https://doi.org/10.15585/mmwr.mm7115a2.

Woldesenbet, Selamawit A., Tendesayi Kufa, Peter Barron, Brian C. Chirombo, Mireille Cheyip, Kassahun Ayalew, Carl Lombard et al. 'Viral Suppression and Factors Associated with Failure to Achieve Viral Suppression among Pregnant Women in South Africa'. *AIDS* 34, no. 4 (2020): 589–597. https://doi.org/10.1097/qad.0000000000002457.

Worldometer. *COVID-19 Coronavirus Pandemic: Coronavirus Cases.* 2023. https://www.worldometers.info/coronavirus/. Accessed 31 May 2023.

Zhou, Peng and Zheng-Li Shi. 'SARS-COV-2 Spillover Events'. *Science* 371, no. 6525 (2021): 120–122. https://doi.org/10.1126/science.abf6097.

Zhu, Tuofu, Bette T. Korber, Andre J. Nahmias, Edward Hooper, Paul M. Sharp and David D. Ho. 'An African HIV-1 Sequence from 1959 and Implications for the Origin of the Epidemic'. *Nature* 391, no. 6667 (1998): 594–597. https://doi.org/10.1038/35400.

Zimmermann, Marita, Brittany Hagedorn and Hil Lyons. 'Projection of Costs of Polio Eradication Compared to Permanent Control'. *The Journal of Infectious Diseases* 221, no. 4 (2019): 561–565. https://doi.org/10.1093/infdis/jiz488.

INDEX